MOZART

A BICENTENNIAL TRIBUTE

MOZART

A BICENTENNIAL TRIBUTE

WENDY THOMPSON

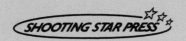

A QUANTUM BOOK

Published by Shooting Star Press, Inc.
230 Fifth Avenue, Suite 1212
New York, NY 10001
USA

ISBN 1-57335-467-8

This book was produced by
Quantum Books Ltd
6 Blundell Street
London N7 9BH

Printed in China by Leefung-Asco Printers Ltd

Contents

I
Musician and Man

Ask any musician who the world's greatest composer is, and the answer will probably be: 'Apart from Mozart, . . .' To the non-musician, the name Mozart means the archetypal prodigy, the boy who started composing at four years old, and as a child touring the courts of Europe astounded monarchs with his amazing aptitude for keyboard playing; who at 14 copied out from memory a complex choral piece heard once in the Sistine Chapel; who died in mysterious circumstances and was given a pauper's funeral in an unmarked grave. What is it about Wolfgang Amadeus Mozart that places him on an artistic par with Shakespeare or Rembrandt, a giant of his art? Any discussion of his life must inevitably start with the legacy of his music which, 200 years later, still moves, delights, fascinates, and astounds us.

In the course of his short life – 35 years – Mozart wrote over 600 pieces of music in all the forms and styles of his day. Unlike JS Bach (arguably his greatest predecessor), whose music sprang from a single, overriding impulse – his deep religious beliefs – Mozart was able to take the common musical currency of his day, sacred or secular – opera, symphony, concerto, Mass, string quartet, sonata – and turn it into pure gold. Every musical form which passed through his hands emerged immeasurably the richer. Who now has ever heard the operas of Koželuh, Graun, Hasse, Salieri, even of Joseph Haydn, Mozart's greatest contemporary, and his only serious rival? Of Mozart's 17 completed operas, *The Marriage of Figaro, Don Giovanni, Così fan tutte,* and *The Magic Flute* are today in the repertory of every opera company in the world. In structure, sense of drama, depth of characterization, and innate understanding of the singer's art, they have never been equalled, and they represent the touchstone by which all later operas have been judged. Then, whereas the concertos of Haydn represent a tiny and relatively insignificant fraction of his output, three of Mozart's five violin concertos rank among the 'top ten' works in that repertory; his magnificent Clarinet Concerto has never been surpassed; his concertos for horn and flute are still among the finest works for their

ABOVE *Leopold Mozart with his two children, Wolfgang and Nannerl, in court dress; watercolour by Louis Carrogis de Carmontelle. This is one of several versions of the same subject; the original was painted in 1763.*

respective instruments; while he may without exaggeration be said to have 'invented' the piano concerto as we know it, with his 23 original masterpieces in the genre. In the field of the symphony, there was rather more competition. Here Haydn was the principal pioneer, but Mozart expanded the form, pushing it to its limits within the Classical framework he inherited, and laying the foundation for the supreme achievements of Beethoven. With due humility, Mozart recorded another debt to Haydn by dedicating to the older composer the six finest of his 23 string quartets. Mozart's 17 piano sonatas also show Haydn's influence, but, like much of his music, works such as No 8 in A minor and No 14 in C minor betray a depth of emotion which only rarely invests Haydn's music. Added to these basic categories are quantities of dances, serenades, church music, concert arias, songs and chamber music, some of them functional and unexceptional, others individual masterworks – the Sinfonia Concertante for violin and viola, the C minor Mass, the motet *Ave verum corpus*, the unfinished *Requiem*, the four great string quintets, the Clarinet Quintet and the Quintet for piano and wind. Even many of his contributions to contemporary entertainment music – serenades and divertimentos – transcend their original function to reveal such gems as the 'Haffner' Serenade, the exquisite miniature *Eine Kleine Nachtmusik* and the three magnificent wind serenades, in B flat, E flat, and C minor.

What makes Mozart's music unique? Today it is beyond our comprehension that *The Marriage of Figaro* could have been greeted with indifference in Vienna, that a relatively sophisticated musical public could fail to appreciate and cherish such talent. Mozart worked with the commonplace musical fabric of his time, the prescribed structures, instrumental combinations, harmonic progressions and melodic formulae that he had absorbed as a child, and from which a Salieri and hundreds like him fashioned polite, two-dimensional drawing-room music suitable for the delectation or titillation of many a jaded aristocratic ear. In Mozart's hands this univeral *galant* language emerged transmuted into structures of awesome perfection, clothed in phrases of searing beauty, and invested with an expressive power capable of illuminating the entire range of human emotions. Quite simply, it surpassed any requirements. 'Too many notes, my dear Mozart', the baffled Emperor Joseph II is said to have remarked on leaving the première of *Die Entführung aus dem Serail*. Like the secret of Stradivari's varnish, this extra dimension defies analysis. We can only call it genius.

Mozart's musical development was, naturally, shaped by the circumstances of his life. He was born at a time when the great majority of musicians were employed by patrons – wealthy aristocrats, monarchs, or prelates – or as civic musicians working for a town council. As such, they were treated as menials, on a level with cooks, footmen and other servants. Mozart's own father Leopold, and later Wolfgang

ABOVE *Wolfgang Mozart (1756–91); anonymous portrait.*

himself, worked for the Archbishop of Salzburg, for whom they were required to produce music for ceremonial and sacred occasions, and also for the personal diversion of their patron. Until he was finally pensioned off, Haydn spent nearly all his working life in the service of the powerful Esterházy family. Fortunately, Prince Nikolaus Esterházy was an enlightened and civilized person, who appreciated Haydn's outstanding abilities, and allowed him a certain degree of freedom to pursue his own interests. Nevertheless, such a post had its drawbacks: the prince could detain his musicians at will, and, on one occasion, Haydn was obliged to drop his patron a heavy hint – in the form of the 'Farewell' Symphony – that the court orchestra members had been kept away from their families in Vienna for too long. Such a patron could, of course, also dictate what 'his' composer should write: Prince Nikolaus' own favourite instrument was an archaic and unwieldy form of viola da gamba, called a baryton. In the course of his service, poor Haydn was obliged to compose no less than 126 trios for this instrument, purely for the prince's amusement.

This kind of life – secure (so long as the patron was kept happy) but strictly limited – did not appeal to Mozart. By the early 1780s the spirit of the Enlightenment, emphasizing individual freedom and status, was filtering through to Austria from pre-Revolutionary France. To the great distress of his father, a natural conformist who was most anxious to secure a permanent post for his brilliant son, Wolfgang decided to shake off the shackles of patronage, and leave provincial Salzburg to go freelance in cosmopolitan Vienna. There he intended to earn a living giving concerts, composing to various commissions from different sources, and teaching. At first he made a great success of his new-found freedom, earning sufficient money to rent an elegant apartment, marry, and enjoy a reasonable standard of living. But once his novelty value had worn off among the blasé Viennese, his audiences declined, while jealousy and court intrigue combined to deny him the court appointments and lucrative commissions he so desperately needed. His output in these later years shows that he made every effort to adapt to changing economic circumstances: Austria was then at war with the Ottoman Empire, and the war effort had begun to drain the financial resources of the upper-class patrons on whose support Mozart relied. As concerts became fewer and more difficult to fill, he turned to writing music suitable for publication – fewer large-scale works such as symphonies and piano concertos, and more chamber music suitable for domestic consumption. But very little – if any – was written as pure speculation. The Romantic ideal of the free artist, creating from inner conviction, was not far off, but for Mozart it had not yet arrived.

Mozart was by no means the first freelance composer to die in financial difficulties in the days before copyright law and performance rights afforded the artist some protection: 60 years later the German composer Gustav Lortzing literally starved to death after having to sell his

ABOVE *Mozart's sister Maria Anna Mozart (1751–1829); she was always known as 'Nannerl'.*

hugely successful operas to publishers for a pitifully inadequate outright fee, which denied him any further revenue. But for a while Mozart proved that life as a freelance was possible, and others after him – the tougher and more astute Beethoven, for example – took advantage of the possibilities opened up by Mozart's mould-breaking career.

Earlier biographies tend to suffer from the 'he was a genius therefore he must have been a saint' syndrome. They have been particularly hard on Leopold Mozart, who is portrayed as a stern, tyrannical disciplinarian, dragging the little boy and his gifted sister round Europe like a pair of performing monkeys, constantly nagging at his adolescent son, and finally growing old and bitter alone in Salzburg after Wolfgang had left for Vienna and married against his father's wishes. Also singled out for particular censure has been Mozart's wife Constanze, who has often been accused of hastening her husband's early death through her sluttishness, extravagance, and inability to keep the household finances in order. Mozart, in contrast, is held up as a kind of plaster saint, a spiritual being who lived through his music, pausing only for the occasional game of billiards. A quite different view is taken by Peter Shaffer's celebrated play *Amadeus:* his Mozart is childishly obscene, irritating, giggly, obnoxiously puffed-up with self-importance, and supremely tactless. The truth, as might be guessed, probably lies somewhere in between.

Mozart's life and character are well documented by the extensive correspondence that was generated within his family by his frequent travels and we are given a fascinating glimpse into matters both artistic and domestic. The personality which emerges is amazingly ordinary and down-to-earth. Unlike Beethoven's, Mozart's was no Promethean spirit struggling with the complex moral and intellectual issues of his day. On the contrary, he was very much concerned with material things, sharing the contemporary view of his art as a craft, which would afford him material success as well as artistic fulfilment. Even his involvement with Freemasonry was probably dictated more by practical considerations than by any close identification with the higher spiritual aims of the movement. To be called 'brother' by the cream of Viennese society was no doubt a necessary step on the ladder of social advancement.

Mozart was himself very much aware of his own unique talents, but they did not correspond with any unique saintliness of character. He tended to be rather naïve in his dealings with others; outspokenly critical, to the point of rudeness, of his less gifted fellow-musicians – a trait which was to earn him many enemies; deceitful on occasion; and certainly arrogant, in an age when obsequiousness and servile flattery were necessary to ensure success. This lack of the courtier's innate instinct for self-preservation – a characteristic he shared with his father – did not endear him to the aristocracy, and probably lost him the appointments he needed. Nevertheless, he was honest enough to give credit where it was due: he had great respect for Johann Christian Bach (son of Johann Sebastian), whom he met in London as a child; Joseph Haydn, whom he revered above all other contemporaries; and a few others less well-known today.

The Mozarts were clearly a happy and affectionate family. Wolfgang and his sister Nannerl remained on close terms throughout his life: his early letters to her and to a Salzburg cousin, Anna Maria Thekla ('the Bäsle', as he called her) are full of juvenile high spirits, spiced with an earthy, often indelicate sense of humour, while his later letters to his sister show a touching solicitude for the state of her health and spirits. But the two crucial relationships of his life were with his father and, later, with his wife.

Leopold Mozart was totally devoted to his brilliant son, whose extraordinary talents he recognized from the start. In those days, children were not so sheltered as now from the pressures of adult life, and the exploitation of child prodigies for material gain was not frowned upon. Leopold felt it his duty to further Wolfgang's career from the start at the expense of his own. There is no evidence that Wolfgang resented the many and arduous journeys he was obliged to undertake in the pursuit of fame and success: on the contrary, he seems to have enjoyed seeing new places, meeting new people, and showing off his manifold abilities, despite the inevitable detrimental effect of all this on his health. However, once Leopold relinquished his role of chaperone and travelling companion and the adolescent Wolfgang found himself off the parental leash, he promptly set about indulging all his hitherto repressed impulses, just like any other high-spirited teenager. The ill-fated Mannheim–Paris trip of 1778, which Mozart undertook with his mother, not with Leopold, marked the end of the close, trusting relationship that father and son had formerly enjoyed. Leopold had been forced to come to terms with several disagreeable flaws in his son's character, including his alarming capacity to be 'economical with the truth' when circumstances demanded. Their relationship was further strained when Wolfgang threw security to the winds to go to Vienna, and it suffered irreparable damage when a new and more powerful force – in the form of a prospective bride – entered Wolfgang's life. Leopold realized that he would have no further influence over his son's career. The tale is all too familiar, but in this case it has a tragic poignancy: Leopold's heart was broken by his son's defection, and the rift between them remained unhealed even at the old man's death.

The much maligned Constanze seems to have played a more dominant role in Mozart's later life than many biographers have given her credit for. By no means the ignorant slut often portrayed, she was on the contrary a capable organizer, well able to discuss music intelligently with her husband and of managing their financial affairs – even the disgruntled Leopold was forced to admit that the household management showed every sign of prudence. The couple clearly enjoyed a

ABOVE *Leopold Mozart (1719–88); anonymous portrait.*

passionate, tender and loving marriage, as Mozart's touchingly intimate letters to his 'dearest, best loved little wife' testify. One of the reasons why Constanze did not really come into her own until after Mozart's death may well have been that she spent much of her married life in various debilitating stages of pregnancy, bearing six children (of whom only two survived). Her own health suffered greatly, which caused Mozart much anxiety. Certainly Constanze and Wolfgang seem to have gained more satisfaction from their marital relationship than from parenthood: on two occasions they abandoned a newly born baby to the mercies of a wet-nurse while they undertook a prolonged journey; and, while Mozart occasionally refers affectionately to his eldest son in his letters, the little boy was sent away to school as soon as possible, presumably to give his father some peace to work. It seems that Constanze supplied Mozart with the sexual fulfilment he needed, and, although rumours abounded at the time, and have continued ever since, that both husband and wife took other lovers, there is not a shred of evidence to support such a theory.

Physically, Mozart was a small, slight man, about 5ft 4in (1.6m) tall. He had very fine, fair hair and pale skin, faintly pitted by smallpox. Nannerl said he was handsome as a child, but lost his looks in later life. Several authentic portraits exist, of which the unfinished one by his brother-in-law Joseph Lange (*see* page 65), painted about two years before Mozart's death, is said to be the most accurate likeness. His friend Michael Kelly described how, when he became animated, his whole face lit up in a way 'as impossible to describe, as it would be to paint sunbeams'.

OPPOSITE *This posthumous portrait of Mozart was painted by Barbara Krafft in 1819, 28 years after the composer's death, and yet is considered to be a true likeness.*

II
'The miracle God let be born in Salzburg'

'I<small>T WAS 25 YEARS AGO</small>, I think', wrote Leopold Mozart to his wife on their wedding anniversary in 1772, 'that we had the bright idea of getting married.' The son of a bookbinder from Augsburg, Leopold had studied philosophy at the Benedictine university in Salzburg, but the academic life did not suit him, and he was expelled in 1739. By 1747, the year of his marriage to the cheerful and practical Salzburger, Maria Anna Pertl, he was working as fourth violinist in the court orchestra of the prince-archbishop of Salzburg. Leopold's own career progressed slowly and unadventurously: by 1758 he had risen up the ranks to become second violin, and also court and chamber composer, and five years later he became deputy kapellmeister (the German term for the musician in charge of a musical establishment). By this time he had published a major treatise on violin technique, and had fathered seven children, of whom only two, a daughter and a son, survived. The last of these – the child whose birth his father described as a 'God-given miracle' – was Wolfgang Amadeus Mozart.

Born on 27 January, 1756 (the feast of St John Chrysostom), in a house on the Getreidegasse, the boy was christened Joannes Chrysostomus Wolfgangus Theophilus. The last of his names, Greek for 'beloved of God', came from his godfather, but in later life Mozart used the Latin form 'Amadeus'. His parents might have done well to remember the ancient adage, 'Those whom the gods love die young'.

Wolfgang's elder sister Maria Anna (always known as Nannerl) began to learn the harpsichord in 1758, when she was seven, and quickly showed exceptional talent. But her little brother took to the instrument himself at the age of four, and soon learnt some of Nannerl's pieces. By the time he was five, he had, with his father's help, composed a couple of short keyboard pieces himself. This was enough to convince Leopold that he had a potential prodigy on his hands. By 1761 Leopold had made a crucial decision – to give up both violin teaching and composition in order to devote all his spare time to furthering the careers and education of his children. With this in

ABOVE *Mozart's mother, Maria Anna, née Pertl (1720–78)*

ABOVE *Mozart's birthplace in Salzburg.*

14

ABOVE A *view of Salzburg.*

mind, he introduced Wolfgang to the public at a concert at Salzburg university in the autumn of 1761, and then set about arranging the first of their many international tours. In January and February 1762 he took Nannerl and Wolfgang to Munich, where they both played to the Elector of Bavaria. Later the same year the whole family set off for Vienna, where the children played to the Empress Maria Theresia and her consort at the beautiful Schönbrunn palace. The six-year-old Wolfgang – 'a lively, spirited, charming child' – was a great success, exciting universal admiration. He also amused everyone by cheekily proposing marriage to the empress's six-year-old daughter, Maria Antonia – the future Queen of France. But Maria Theresia was sufficiently impressed to present the family with a stylish set of court clothes: Nannerl's was the court dress of an archduchess, of white brocaded taffeta, richly ornamented, while Wolfgang received a lily-coloured suit with broad gold trimmings. Their proud father had them painted wearing their new finery.

After their return to Salzburg, Wolfgang's aptitude for music developed daily. By the time he was seven he had 'perfect pitch'; he could also improvise on the keyboard in various styles, play with the keys hidden under a cloth, sight-read anything he was given, add a bass line to a tune, and had 'taught himself' the violin (although such a claim should perhaps be treated with some scepticism – his father after all was a violin teacher). His musical memory was so acute that he once confounded a friend of his father's, the court trumpeter and violinist Johann Andreas Schachtner, by insisting that Schachtner's violin had been tuned exactly an eighth of a tone (a tiny but noticeable fraction) lower than Wolfgang's own when he had last heard it – a fact that the astonished Schachtner was able to verify. But despite Wolfgang's amazing prowess, he remained a docile, industrious and affectionate child, remarkably unspoilt by all the adulation he received.

After only four months at home, Leopold decided to set out on another, longer tour, this time to Paris and London. The family stopped at major towns along the route – Munich, Augsburg, Ludwigsburg, Schwetzingen, Mainz, Frankfurt and Koblenz – for the children to give concerts and to play privately for the aristocracy. Rather than the hoped-for cash, they were showered with snuffboxes and other trinkets,

LEFT *Mozart, aged 6, playing to the Imperial family at Schönbrunn in 1762.*

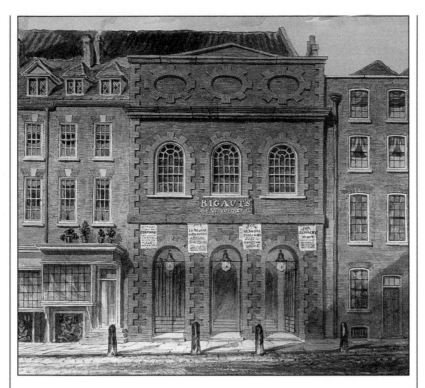

OPPOSITE ABOVE *The Royal Italian Opera House, Covent Garden, London.*

OPPOSITE BELOW *Versailles from the Pièce d'Eau des Suisses; painting by Justin Ouvrie.*

LEFT *The first Opera House in the Haymarket, London, which was later burnt down in 1789.*

to Leopold's disgust: at Aachen, Princess Anna Amalia considered a regal kiss sufficient reward. Finally, the travel-stained family arrived in Paris, where they were befriended by various members of the intellectual set, especially the German Baron Grimm. It was he who arranged their introduction to the French court. On New Year's Day 1764 the Mozart children played before Louis XV at Versailles, and were allowed to stand behind the royal family at a state banquet. It was in Paris that Wolfgang's first compositions appeared in print – four sonatas for keyboard and violin, containing one of 'unusual *goût*', as Leopold reported proudly to his Salzburg landlord. 'God works new miracles daily in this infant.'

From Paris, the Mozarts crossed the Channel to England – no light undertaking in those days. In London, their friendly reception at the court of George III and his German-born wife Queen Charlotte was in complete contrast to the snobbery of Versailles. London in the 1760s was a cultured and musically sophisticated centre. The Hanoverian monarchs were great patrons of the arts, and actively promoted the music of both native-born and Continental musicians. Handel had been dead for five years, but his music was still enormously popular; JC Bach (whose concert series run by himself and his compatriot Carl Friedrich Abel was one of the highlights of musical life at the time) was also music master to the queen and a member of her private chamber band: as such he was responsible for organizing elaborate concerts at court. At the major theatres – the King's, the Little Theatre in the Haymarket, Covent Garden and Drury Lane – audiences could enjoy the best of contemporary Italian opera, together with works by British composers like Arne, Hook and Dibdin. This was also the heyday of the pleasure garden, where in the pleasantly pastoral atmosphere of Marylebone, Vauxhall and Ranelagh, the public were treated to promenades, food, firework displays and all manner of other entertainments, naturally including music – such as the works of the best Continental symphonists, songs, little theatrical performances, and organ concertos.

Such was the musical milieu into which the young Wolfgang arrived in 1764. He was quickly invited to play at court, where he delighted the king by playing at sight pieces by JC Bach, Abel, and (George III's favourite) Handel; playing brilliantly on the organ; accompanying Queen Charlotte in an aria; and improvising a melody over a Handelian bass. Leopold reported that everyone was amazed. Furthermore, the English were quick to show their appreciation in hard cash – 24 guineas for a court appearance, 100 for a public concert. This was better than snuffboxes. Wolfgang also appeared at Ranelagh Gardens, playing some of his own pieces on the organ and harpsichord. Such was the incredulity which greeted this phenomenal eight-year-old that, in order to dispel rumours of fraud, Leopold invited the eminent philosopher and member of the Royal Society, Daines Barrington, to put Wolfgang's talents to the test. Barrington reported that the boy could

OPPOSITE ABOVE Covent Garden Market, London, in the 1760s; painting by John Collet.

OPPOSITE BELOW A view of the River Thames at Lambeth Palace; painting by Thomas Priest, c1760.

BELOW Vauxhall Gardens, London; coloured aquatint by Thomas Rowlandson.

indeed perform all the feats with which he was credited, including the
ability to improvise operatic arias in any given style on the harpsichord.

The Mozarts' stay in London was both happy and successful. Wolfgang spent a great deal of time in the company of JC Bach, with whom
he struck up a friendship, and who was delighted to engage in amicable
improvisation contests on the keyboard. The only cloud to appear on the
horizon was Leopold's unexpected illness, which obliged the family to
move out of town to the peaceful, then almost rural atmosphere of
Ebury Street in Pimlico. There, in order not to disturb his convales-
cent father, Wolfgang abandoned practice in favour of composition,
and his earliest symphonies were probably written there. These show a

remarkable grasp of the prevalent styles of the time that were adopted by both Italian and English composers, and especially by JC Bach.

The family left London with genuine regret, having been pressed to stay. Their homeward journey took them via Lille (where Wolfgang fell ill), Ghent, Antwerp and The Hague (where they gave two public concerts and played, by special request, to the Princess of Weilburg, to whom Wolfgang dedicated a set of six keyboard and violin sonatas). Both children then fell seriously ill with typhoid fever: Nannerl nearly died. Wolfgang recovered sufficiently to give two concerts in Amsterdam where his new symphony (No 5 in B flat, K.22, written in The Hague) was played. Once the children were fully fit, the family went on to Paris, where they stayed for two months. There Baron Grimm heard Wolfgang again, and marvelled at his remarkable prowess. Even after such a long absence from home, Leopold could not bear to waste any opportunity of showing off his brilliant children, so, instead of going straight back to Salzburg, they took a tortuous route through Dijon, Lyons, Switzerland, Donaueschingen and Augsburg to Munich, where Leopold even contemplated extending the trip to Italy. But Wolfgang fell ill once more, and the plan was called off. On 30 November 1766, having been away for over three years, the Mozarts returned to Salzburg. It must have been good to be home.

OPPOSITE A view of Amsterdam, where Mozart's symphony No 5 in B flat was first performed in 1765.

BELOW Mozart, seated at the harpsichord, playing at the Prince de Conti's tea-party in Paris in 1766; oil painting by Michel Barthélemy Ollivier.

III
Vienna and Italy

OVER THE NEXT NINE MONTHS, Wolfgang stayed at home in Salzburg, learning arithmetic (which he enjoyed), Latin, and Italian in preparation for the next trip. Musically the interim was not unproductive: he compiled several keyboard concertos from other composers' music collected in Paris and London, and made his first foray into vocal music, with a couple of Italian arias; he composed a comedy in Latin for Salzburg university entitled *Apollo et Hyacinthus*, a piece of Passion music, and the first act of a sacred Singspiel, *Die Schuldigkeit des ersten Gebots*, written in collaboration with Joseph Haydn's younger brother Michael (who since 1762 had been music director to the Archbishop of Salzburg) and another local composer, Jacob Adlgasser.

In September 1767 Leopold took his family once more to Vienna, where festivities were in preparation for the wedding of an archduchess. Unfortunately, the bride-to-be died in a smallpox epidemic, which plunged the city both into mourning and quarantine. The Mozarts retreated to the city of Brünn (now Brno in Czechoslovakia), and then to Olmütz (now Olomouc), where both children contracted smallpox. Though both survived, Wolfgang suffered some facial disfigurement. By January 1768 they were back in Vienna, where Leopold had set his heart on securing an opera commission for Wolfgang. No composer was considered worthy of the name until he had written an opera, which was then regarded as representing the peak of musical achievement. Contemporary operas fell into three main categories: *opera seria*, a genre of high moral – sometimes tragic – tone, dealing usually with heroic or mythological subjects, and suitable for court productions; *opera buffa*, its comic equivalent, dealing with more everyday subject matter (both had texts in Italian); and vernacular opera, usually farcical in nature, with spoken dialogue in the appropriate country's tongue – in Germany and Austria, this was known as Singspiel.

Leopold's plan to persuade the authorities at the Viennese court to commission an opera from Wolfgang (which he boasted was the

OPPOSITE *Michael Haydn (1737–1806), the younger brother of Joseph Haydn, was the music director to the Archbishop of Salzburg from 1762 and a friend of the Mozarts; anonymous artist.*

RIGHT *Nannerl Mozart as a child; oil painting attributed to Pietro Antonio Lorenzoni, 1763.*

RIGHT *Thomas Linley (1756–78) with his sister Elizabeth; oil painting by Thomas Gainsborough, 1768. Mozart met Thomas, another musical prodigy, in Florence in 1770, where they played violin duets together and engaged in friendly rivalry.*

emperor's own idea) soon ran into determined opposition from vested interests – Wolfgang's first real taste of professional jealousy. Leopold bitterly denounced this 'conspiracy'. 'The whole musical inferno has risen up to stop a child's brilliance being seen', he wrote. But there was a consolation prize: Wolfgang's little Singspiel *Bastien und Bastienne* – a tale of thwarted love put right by the intervention of a sorcerer – was performed privately at the home of Dr Mesmer, the celebrated inventor of magnetic mesmerism (which Mozart was later to parody in *Così fan tutte*). He was also invited to conduct a Mass of his own before the imperial court, which, according to Leopold, went some way towards repairing the damage their enemies had done by preventing the opera.

Back home, Wolfgang set about writing the opera anyway. *La finta semplice* (The Pretended Simpleton), an *opera buffa* based on a play by Goldoni, was duly performed in the Archbishop of Salzburg's palace theatre on 1 May 1769, to the satisfaction of its 13-year-old composer.

During this year Mozart added to his expanding list of works another Mass (K.66) and other sacred works, dance pieces, and three orchestral serenades, called *Cassations*, for the end-of-term festivities at the university. The archbishop rewarded Wolfgang with the title of konzertmeister.

Leopold was soon restless again. Italy – the promised land for any musician, particularly a potential opera composer – beckoned, and in December 1769, father and son set out alone. Poor Nannerl, at 18 now too old to be considered a child prodigy, was left at home with her mother: her concert-giving days were over. For the next 15 years she was to lead an undistinguished life of secluded domesticity until her marriage to a middle-aged magistrate, by whom she bore three children.

Leopold and Wolfgang followed their usual pattern of stopping at large towns, such as Innsbruck, Rovereto, Verona and Mantua, to give concerts and to allow sceptics to subject Wolfgang's legendary abilities to stringent tests. By the end of January they were in Milan, where they were befriended by the Austrian governor-general, Count Firmian. He arranged several important introductions to, among

LEFT *Padre Giovanni Battista Martini (1706–84), the brilliant theorist whom Mozart met in Bologna in 1770.*

LEFT *Mozart at the keyboard in Verona; oil painting by Saverio dalla Rosa, 1770.*

others, the composers G. B. Sammartini and Piccinni (respectively leading lights in the instrumental and operatic fields). The Italians welcomed the young prodigy, and an opera commission was quickly arranged, although Leopold was pessimistic about their chances of making any money: 'We shall have to content ourselves with admiration and applause instead.'

Wolfgang's letters home to his mother and sister are full of childish prattle about the places they visited and the people they met, such as the remarkable singer Lucrezia Aguiari – 'La Bastardella' – who could dispatch incredibly high notes with effortless ease. By late March they were in Bologna, where Wolfgang was put through his paces by the famous theorist Padre Martini, who professed himself amazed at the boy's ability to work out complex fugues on a brief given subject. In Florence, Wolfgang met his English contemporary, Thomas Linley – another supremely gifted prodigy who was to die tragically young (he was drowned at the age of 21). The two boys got on remarkably well, playing violin duets, and engaging in friendly contests of virtuosity. According to Leopold, young Thomas wept bitterly when the time came to part.

From Florence, the Mozarts went on to Rome for Holy Week. It was there that Wolfgang performed one of his celebrated feats of memory by writing out Allegri's famous *Miserere* for double choir, having heard it only once. (No copies of the music were allowed outside the Sistine Chapel.) While in Rome Wolfgang also wrote two more symphonies, both in D major, in the Italian style. From mid-May to mid-June the Mozarts stayed in Naples, where they visited Vesuvius and Pompeii, went to the opera at the beautiful San Carlo theatre, and were received by the King and Queen of Naples. Back in Rome, Wolfgang was made a Knight of the Order of the Golden Spur by the pope – a higher distinction than that conferred on the Viennese court kapellmeister, Gluck. Further honours awaited him at Bologna, where he applied for membership of the Accademia Filarmonica. His entrance test was to set a four-part antiphon (in a locked room to prevent cheating): he completed the task – which took some composers four hours or so – in just over half an hour, and was unanimously elected a member of the Accademia.

Back in Milan, Wolfgang set to work on his new opera *Mitridate, rè di Ponto* (Mitridate, King of Pontus), based on a play by Racine. Despite a few last-minute rewritings of arias and the customary professional intrigues among the singers, the opera's première at the Regio Ducale theatre on 26 December 1770 was a great success. According to Leopold, several arias were encored, and almost all elicited 'great applause'.

Flushed with success, Leopold and Wolfgang left Milan in mid-January 1771 to return home to Salzburg. Mozart had received several new commissions: an opera for Milan for 1772, an oratorio, *La Betulia*

ABOVE Florence from near
San Miniato; J M W Turner.
The Mozart family stayed
briefly in Florence in the spring
of 1770 before moving on to
Rome for Holy Week.

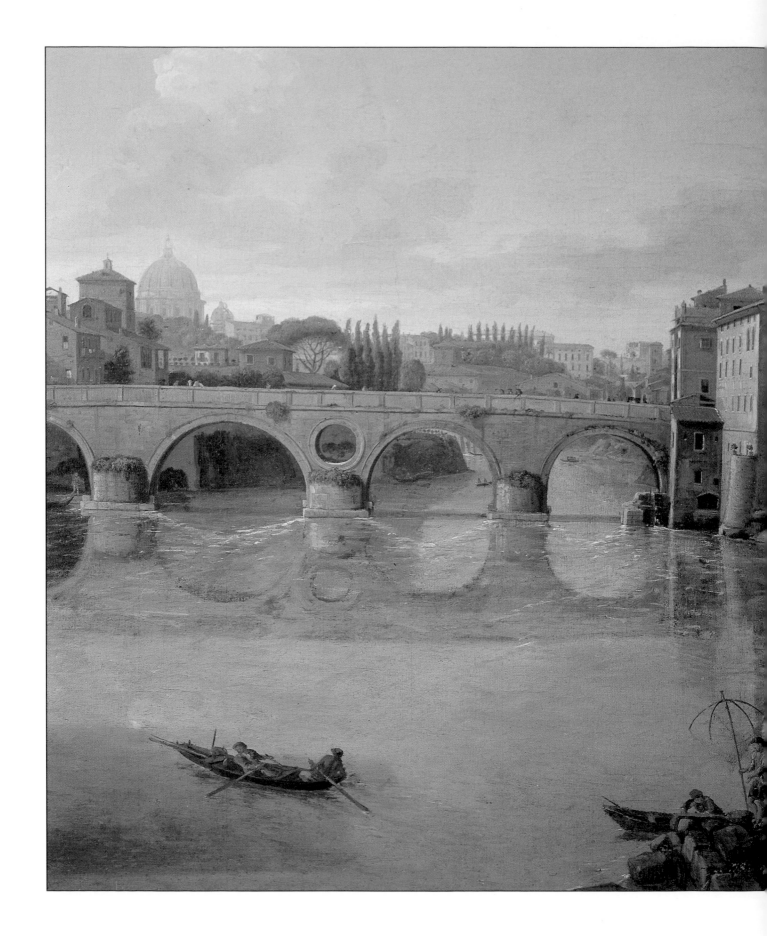

FAR LEFT *The Ponte Sisto, Rome; painting by Caspar van Wittel.*

LEFT *Mozart wearing the Papal Order of the Golden Spur; anonymous portrait. Mozart was presented with this notable distinction by the pope in Rome in 1770.*

liberata, for Padua, and a serenata for performance in Milan in October 1771 to celebrate the marriage of Maria Theresia's son the Archduke Ferdinand. After a brief period at home, he and Leopold returned in August to Milan, where Wolfgang finished the serenata *Ascanio in Alba*. It was well received and had several performances. But here Wolfgang experienced the first of many official rebuttals. He applied for a post in the service of the archduke: but Ferdinand was advised by his mother not to burden himself with such 'useless creatures who travel around all over the place, like beggars'. After giving a concert in early December, the Mozarts decided to return to Salzburg.

Their last Italian journey began ten months later. The new Milanese opera, *Lucio Silla* (another *opera seria*) had been partly written during the summer in Salzburg, but Mozart could not complete it until he had heard each of the principal soloists, and was able to adjust his arias and recitatives to suit individual voices. The première, bedevilled as always by singers' last-minute indispositions, and by the late arrival of the archduke, was nevertheless a success, and the opera had a total of 26 performances. A more enduring product of this last trip was the motet *Exsultate, jubilate*, K.165, written for the principal singer Venanzio Rauzzini (who was a male soprano, one of the many victims of the still prevalent barbaric custom of castrating the most talented boy singers before their voices broke). The motet – sung today, of course, by female sopranos – remains a vocal showpiece, and is one of Mozart's most popular early works. In Milan, he also completed a set of six string quartets, K.155–160, his first real essays in the medium.

Leopold dawdled before setting off for home. He had applied on Wolfgang's behalf for a post with the Grand Duke of Tuscany (another of Maria Theresia's numerous offspring), but after a long delay the reply came back: No. Presumably the grand duke, too, had been warned against these 'useless creatures'. By 13 March 1773 the Mozarts, somewhat disillusioned, were back home. Neither visited Italy again.

IV
Life in Salzburg
1773–1777

LEOPOLD AND WOLFGANG had arrived home after their second Italian trip to a death – that of Leopold's kindly and indulgent employer, Count Schrattenbach, Archbishop of Salzburg. His successor, Hieronymus Colloredo, was a much colder fish – austere, status-conscious, and less inclined to permit his servants to take such liberties as prolonged periods of absence in the furtherance of their own careers. With some misgivings, Wolfgang settled down to work steadily at a stream of compositions, beginning with the Italian serenata *Il sogno di Scipione* (Scipio's Dream) for the ceremonial enthronement of the new archbishop on 14 March 1772. By July, Wolfgang had been rewarded for his efforts with a formal appointment to the post he had filled in an honorary capacity – on and off – for the past three years, that of konzertmeister. His salary – 150 florins a year – was modest, but reasonable for a 16-year-old.

After the rather disappointing end to his adventures in Italy, Wolfgang once more devoted himself to composition – more symphonies, divertimentos for wind instruments, Masses, and a double violin concerto. Leopold, however, was worried. He clearly had strong forebodings about Wolfgang's future in Salzburg: Archbishop Colloredo was not only less tolerant than his predecessor, but unwilling to recognize and appreciate genius, even when it was to be found on his own doorstep. As soon as Colloredo's back was turned, Leopold, in the summer of 1773, took Wolfgang to Vienna hoping for a court appointment. Despite her privately expressed views on the Mozarts, the empress received them courteously enough, but no appointment was forthcoming. However, Wolfgang did acquire some valuable contacts, including the French ballet-master J. G. Noverre, whose radical ideas were currently transforming both the perception and the execution of dance, from a formal, stylized entertainment to a medium for emotional expression. One of Noverre's choreographic masterpieces, *Don Juan* (with music by Gluck), was to have a significant influence on Mozart's own *Don Giovanni*. But the single most important result of the visit was to bring Wolfgang into contact with the music of Joseph Haydn, whose latest set of string quartets, Op.20, had just been published. Stimulated and excited by Haydn's example, Mozart immediately set to work on a similar set, K.168–73, in which denser textures, use of contrapuntal devices, and a more rigorous approach, as opposed to the sensuous, Italianate tunefulness of the earlier set, all point to Haydn's influence. Wolfgang also began his first string quintet, K.174, and completed a serenade containing a mini-violin concerto, in the traditional Salzburg fashion.

Wolfgang spent the rest of 1773 and most of 1774 at home. Of his eight symphonies written over this period, two (No 25 in G minor, K.183, and No 29 in A major, K.201) are works of outstanding maturity, and are his earliest symphonies to take their place in the standard modern repertory. The G minor symphony marks Mozart's first use of this key (then closely associated with the fashionable *Sturm und Drang* – Storm and Stress – style). The colour and mood suggested by individual keys was to become increasingly important to Mozart, who was clearly already more sensitive to particular key associations than were many of his contemporaries. Thus he used the 'bright' keys of D and C major for ceremonial and festive music such as serenades; G and A major for joyous or pastoral pieces; F major for stately, sometimes military-sounding works; and the emotive minor keys – particularly G, D and C minor – for the expression of overwhelming feelings of passion, tragedy or unease. The key of E flat major held a very special significance, as we shall see later.

1773 also saw the composition of Mozart's first original piano concerto, a medium he was to make uniquely his own. K.175 in D is still a relatively lightweight work, but shows an important advance on the earlier 'parodies', written when he was a child. His sacred music of the period bears witness to the new restrictions imposed by the archbishop, who felt that music in the context of a church service should definitely take second place to devotion. Florid, expansive, operatic-style music was out: austerity and brevity were the new order of the day. Colloredo decreed that an entire Mass setting must last no more than 45 minutes. Wolfgang accordingly turned to the *missa brevis* (short Mass), in which the setting is much condensed. In one of these, K.192, he first introduced the famous four-note 'tag' (C, D, F, E) associated with the word *credo* (I believe), which near the end of his life would supply the finale of his last symphony, the 'Jupiter'.

In the summer of 1774 Wolfgang was commissioned to write an *opera buffa* for the next carnival season in Munich. *La finta giardiniera* (The Pretended Gardener) was written in the autumn and premièred with great success on 13 January 1775. Leopold and Wolfgang were received by the Elector and Electress of Bavaria: Wolfgang wrote to his mother that the theatre was packed, and every aria was received with a 'colossal uproar' (that the plot is one of the most thoroughly confused

TOP *Hieronymus, Count Colloredo, Prince-Archbishop of Salzburg (1732–1812); painting by Franz Xaver König, 1772.*

ABOVE *The Empress Maria Theresia of Austria (1717–80); painting by Martin de Meytens (the Younger).*

RIGHT *The city of Salzburg, with the Archbishop's palace on the rock; painting by Philip Hutchins Rogers.*

and incomprehensible ever devised didn't seem to matter). Carnival time in the cosmopolitan atmosphere of Munich also offered other possibilities for diversion. Leopold and Wolfgang went to masked balls and Wolfgang gave several concerts and took part in a contest of keyboard skills with another ex-child prodigy, Ignaz von Beecke, coming off somewhat the worse.

But the round of pleasure could not last indefinitely. By March Wolfgang had resumed his duties at Salzburg with a heavy heart: never had his birthplace seemed so provincial, limited and dull. He yearned for escape to a place and an audience which would appreciate his talents to the full. Although neither of them knew it, the Munich trip was the last expedition that Leopold and Wolfgang would make together. Leopold was doomed to spend the rest of his life in Salzburg, and Wolfgang was not to leave it again for over two more weary years.

But his time was not wasted as his skills matured. Over those years he produced another serenata, *Il rè pastore* (King as Shepherd), to a text by the famous Italian poet Pietro Metastasio (whose texts were set to music countless times all over Europe by the best composers of the time) for a state visit by Archduke Maximilian Franz; another serenade (K.204) written for the traditional end-of-term jollities at the university; and several violin concertos, of which the last three (in G, D and A major) are standard repertoire today. Each abounds in imaginative little surprises – sudden lapses into folk themes or popular dances and even a mock 'Turkish' episode enliven their finales. Mozart probably played them himself, being a highly competent fiddler: we know that they were also played by the Italian konzertmeister at

OPPOSITE *Joseph Haydn (1732–1809); painting by Thomas Hardy.*

RIGHT *Mozart in 1773; medallion painted on ivory.*

TOP *Pietro Metastasio (1698–1782); Mozart's serenata, Il rè pastore, was composed to a text by the well-known Italian poet.*

ABOVE *J C Bach (1735–82), the youngest son of the great composer, had some influence on Mozart's musical development.*

Salzburg, Antonio Brunetti.

In 1776 Mozart turned his attention to the piano concerto, writing four very different works. The first is an uncomplicated piece of no great distinction; the second, K.246 in C, was written for Countess Lützow of Salzburg: the third was a triple concerto written for three members of a wealthy local family, the Lodrons; and the last, K.271 in E flat, was composed for a French lady virtuoso, Mlle Jeunehomme, who happened to be visiting Salzburg. This work is by far the most impressive of the group: the relationship between soloist and orchestra is developed in a most unconventional way, and the C minor slow movement conveys a telling emotional intensity that presages Mozart's later, great works in that key.

As well as these large-scale pieces, Mozart wrote a number of light entertainment pieces: unpretentious divertimentos for a small group of wind instruments (oboes, bassoons and horns) intended to be played outdoors on a summer evening; more substantial serenades for string quartet and two horns written for the delectation of Countess Lodron; a serenade for seven instruments written for Nannerl's name-day; the massive 'Haffner' Serenade for the marriage of Elisabeth Haffner, daughter of a prominent Salzburg merchant (this also contains a violin concerto, incorporating the famous rondo); and two 'echo' serenades – the *Serenata Notturna* for two contrasting groups of instruments, and the *Notturno* for four groups of strings and horns. Both works exploit the possibilities of clever echo effects, and must have been performed out of doors, with each orchestra in a different place.

Mozart's church music – written as part of his duties – includes five more short Masses, of which K.262 is the most substantial: it may have been written for the Easter celebrations at the cathedral in 1776. His liturgical music of this period does not differ noticeably from his secular in style: it is competent, agreeable, and adequate for the occasion. Mozart was no doubt a good Catholic, but his religion did not weigh heavily upon him. Devotion formed part of his life, but not, as in the case of JS Bach, the greatest part.

ABOVE *Salzburg.*

V

'Off you go to Paris'

IN AUGUST 1777, tired of the limitations of his Salzburg post, Wolfgang petitioned the archbishop for his release. Colloredo decided to kill two troublesome birds with one stone, and discharged Leopold too, but after due reflection on both sides Leopold was reinstated. So Wolfgang set off once more, this time with his mother, on a journey which was to lead to Paris – and tragedy.

Their first stop was Munich, where Wolfgang tried to get a job with the elector, but was refused. Nevertheless, in no hurry to leave, he stayed around, playing privately with friends. Poor Leopold at home was clearly pining for his son: in a touching letter he confessed that he felt sad at times, being unable to hear Wolfgang playing the piano and violin, and each time he approached his home he half expected to hear the familiar sound of his son's fiddle. A week or two later, however, he had put such sentimental feelings behind him, and was sternly ordering his son onwards to Augsburg, to make some money. 'Kind words, praise and "bravissimi" don't pay the landlord's bills . . .' Wolfgang and his mother obediently moved on to Augsburg, where Wolfgang gave a concert, visited the well-known manufacturer of fortepianos, Herr Stein, and tried out some of his instruments. He also entertained the monks at the 'Holy Cross' monastery by playing violin concertos to them, including one of his own, and improvising on the organ. He was clearly a great hit with the brethren: the dean was 'beside himself with delight'.

Once out of Leopold's sight, Wolfgang began to enjoy himself without restriction, possibly for the first time in his life. His poor mother lacked her husband's capacity for discipline, and found herself at the mercy of her headstrong son. Wolfgang was now 21 years old, no longer a child, and so far he had devoted his entire life to music. Other urges were now becoming apparent. In Augsburg, he met up with his cousin, Anna Maria Thekla, with whom he struck up a lively – even unbridled – friendship. His subsequent letters to her reveal a side of his personality that Victorian biographers preferred to suppress.

TOP *Augsburg was the second stop on Mozart's progress to Paris with his mother in 1777.*

ABOVE *The National Theatre, Mannheim, where Mozart attended performances of opera during his stay.*

At this point it seems that Wolfgang was interested in matters more scatological than sexual; his humour is of the smutty adolescent variety that was evidently taken for granted in Salzburg middle class society.

Leopold meanwhile was becoming anxious. 'I wish you could find something to do in Mannheim', he wrote. So Wolfgang and his mother moved on to the spacious, elegant town on the Rhine that had been the seat of the Elector Palatine since 1720. There a vast palace, rivalling Versailles in scope, had been built, containing one of the most beautiful opera houses in Europe. The music-loving elector had immediately installed a substantial orchestra, which by 1777 numbered about 45 players. Under the violinists Johann Stamitz and Christian Cannabich, the orchestra had developed an unparalleled reputation for discipline and virtuosity – an 'army of generals', as the English historian Dr Burney described it. 'No orchestra in the world has ever equalled the Mannheim', wrote the poet and composer CF Schubart. 'Its *forte* is a thunderclap, its *crescendo* a torrent, its *diminuendo* a limpid brook babbling into the distance, its *piano* a spring breeze.' The breadth of musical life was stunning – two concerts a week; chamber music sessions, in which the elector himself, who played several instruments, took part; festivals; and all types of opera productions. At

LEFT *View of Munich, the capital of Bavaria; engraving after Canaletto, 1761.*

the time of Mozart's visit the kapellmeister was Ignaz Holzbauer; the Abbé Vogler (a noted musical theorist and rather second-rate composer) was vice-kapellmeister and court chaplain; while Cannabich was in charge of the orchestra.

Mozart immediately found himself among friends, especially Cannabich (for whose 13-year-old daughter he wrote a piano sonata), the oboist Ramm, the flautist Wendling (who was the father of several attractive daughters), and the tenor Raaff. The atmosphere at the court exuded pleasure. The elector was a promiscuous man: one of Wendling's daughters was his ex-mistress, and Mozart wrote that he had been asked to play the piano to the natural children of the elector

RIGHT Marie Antoinette in her bedroom at Versailles; painting by Gauthier d'Agoty.

ABOVE Paris in the 1770s, which Mozart eventually reached in 1778; painting by Louis-Nicolas de Lespinasse.

who were kept nearby in a separate establishment. Mozart decided to enter into the prevailing spirit of the place. In a mock 'confession' to his father, he unwisely described riotous evenings at Cannabich's house, where he amused the company by making up obscene verses (a natural talent of his), and stayed up until after midnight. Leopold was furious. His son appeared to be bent on wasting his talent and his time, earning no money, and falling into disreputable company. His next letter accused Wolfgang of 'fecklessness, thoughtlessness and laziness', which his son was quick to rebut, pointing out that he was trying to obtain a permanent post at Mannheim. He had spoken to the elector about giving lessons to the royal children, for which he was rewarded not with cash, but with a watch (unfortunately, he already had quite a collection of those). He had also made discreet inquiries about a more permanent post, but once again his hopes were dashed. He had evidently acquired, as well as friends, a few influential enemies, notably vice-kapellmeister Vogler, whose playing and compositions Mozart

had been foolish enough to criticize. As a result, he got the same response as he had received at Munich: 'Sorry, no vacancies'.

By now Christmas was fast approaching, and further travel would soon be inadvisable. Wolfgang took the advice of his Mannheim friends – who professed themselves as disappointed as he on his lack of success – and decided to stay on until the spring, moving to cheaper lodgings and taking on a few pupils to earn money. Wendling had a Dutch friend, an amateur flautist, who was willing to pay for some flute music – three concertos and two quartets. In fact, although he accepted the commission, Mozart never completed all the pieces, later confessing that he couldn't stand the flute (but that was many years before *The Magic Flute*). Nevertheless, he pretended to Leopold that he had fulfilled the commission. He then proposed his new plan: that his mother should go back home, and he would continue on to Paris when the weather improved, together with Wendling, Ramm and the bassoonist Ritter.

Leopold was frantic with anxiety. The trip was coming to nothing: Wolfgang was behaving totally irresponsibly, and he was powerless to influence him. The last straw came in January 1778. Wolfgang had fallen in love.

The object of his affections was a young girl with a 'pure and lovely voice'. Aloysia Weber was one of the six children of Fridolin Weber, a singer and copyist at the Mannheim court theatre. Her elder sister Josepha was already a successful dramatic coloratura soprano in Vienna, but by all accounts Aloysia had even more potential talent. Mozart was enraptured. The first Leopold heard of it was when his son coolly informed him that he was accompanying Aloysia and her father for a few days to visit the Princess of Orange at Kircheim-Bolanden, where Aloysia was to sing several arias that Wolfgang had written for her. Then, to Leopold's horror, Wolfgang wrote again, proposing that he should abandon the Paris idea and go instead to Italy with Aloysia and her father in order to try to make Aloysia's name as an operatic soprano. Leopold was apoplectic. In a desperate appeal to his son's conscience he reminded him of all his own personal sacrifices for the furtherance of his son's career. 'It is entirely up to you whether you can gradually raise yourself to the highest position of eminence ever achieved by a musician . . . whether you choose to leave this world having been ensnared by a skirt, forced to lie on straw and shut up with an attic-full of starving children, or whether, after a Christian life, you go full of satisfaction, honour and glory, your family well provided for, and your name revered by all.'

Leopold went on to point out the obvious flaws in Wolfgang's proposal to get an unknown 16-year-old singer accepted in Italy – the graveyard of many an aspiring career – and to accuse him of having betrayed his father's trust. 'Off you go to Paris – and that soon! Find your place among the great – *aut Caesar, aut nihil!*' Wolfgang still

ABOVE *Mozart; watercolour drawing by Augustin de Saint-Aubin, Paris, 1778.*

demurred, writing back in defence of himself and his beloved. But Leopold soon found another source of grievance – the fact that Wolfgang had lied to him over the money he had earned. Having failed to complete the flute music for De Jean, he had only received half the commission fee, a fact he tried to disguise by claiming that life in Mannheim was very expensive. To add insult to injury, he had even turned down paying pupils in order to give free lessons to Aloysia; and with supreme lack of tact he even described how he had begun an aria for the tenor Raaff, only to turn it into one for Aloysia instead. However, he reluctantly agreed to continue his journey to Paris. On 14 March, 1778 Wolfgang and his mother finally left Mannheim, miserable and virtually penniless. Having set off in great style from Salzburg in their own carriage, they were now so impecunious that they were obliged to sell it before the frontier and go on by postchaise. So far, the tour had been an unmitigated disaster.

On 23 March 1778, after a tedious journey, Wolfgang and his mother arrived in Paris, then the cultural centre of Europe. The little girl to whom Wolfgang had impudently proposed marriage when they were children was now Queen of France; and tales of her extravagant lifestyle at the glittering court of Versailles were stirring up murmurs of discontent among ordinary Frenchmen, setting alight a fuse which 11 years

ABOVE A *Parisian street scene, with mountebanks and promenaders by the Seine.*

later was to blow not only France but much of Europe apart. Meanwhile, however, the rich followed their king's dictum 'Après moi, le déluge', and gave themselves up to pleasure – balls, the opera (where new works by Gluck, Grétry and Piccinni were finally displacing the heroic works of Lully and Rameau, beloved of the Ancien Régime), gambling and hunting; the chattering middle classes were busy discussing politics and aesthetics; writers such as Voltaire and Diderot were chipping away at the foundations of society with their radical ideas of universal fraternity in this 'Age of Enlightenment'; and the poor were being told to 'eat cake', if they had no bread. In this turbulent cauldron, Mozart, a mere foreigner, naïvely expected to make his fortune.

He immediately set about making contacts, with Baron Grimm and other German expatriates; but, as before, he quickly ran up against snobbery, xenophobia and intrigue. In a letter to Leopold he described how he was kept waiting in an icy antechamber for half an hour by the Duchesse de Chabot, to whom he was to play the clavier: when he did play, the assembled company completely ignored him, and continued to sketch. 'Paris', wrote Wolfgang, 'is much altered. The French are not so polite as they were 15 years ago. Their manners now border on the vulgar, and they are terribly arrogant.'

Wolfgang was asked to write some music for the prestigious Concert Spirituel, the most important concert society in Paris. He supplied several choruses for a Miserere by another composer, together with a sinfonia concertante (a popular type of multiple concerto) for his Mannheim friends Wendling (flute), Ritter (bassoon), Ramm (oboe) and Giovanni Punto (horn). What happened to this piece is still an unsolved mystery. Wolfgang told Leopold that he was obliged to write the piece at great speed, and that the four soloists were 'completely in love with it'. The manuscript was then passed to the director of the Concert Spirituel for copying; but the copying was never done and the work never performed. (The Sinfonia Concertante in E flat for oboe, clarinet, bassoon and horn which is played today under Mozart's name appeared only in the 19th century: some of the music may be Mozart's, but the work is clearly a later compilation.) Wolfgang suspected an intrigue. Leopold wrote resignedly, telling him that such things were inevitable for every artist of outstanding talent. Wolfgang intended to write an opera for Paris, but Leopold warned him to study the national taste first, since his reputation would hang on his first piece. 'Do not work in a hurry . . . do nothing for nothing, and see that you get paid for everything.'

In order to survive, he took on a few composition pupils, including the daughter of the Duc de Guines, who was an outstanding flautist and harpist. Dedicated to her is the charming Double Concerto for flute and harp, K.299. He was also offered the post of organist at Versailles, on condition that he spent six months of the year there, but, after some reflection, he turned it down, arousing Leopold's

ABOVE **The market place and Fountain of the Innocents, Paris; painting by J J Chalon.**

anxieties once more. In June some ballet music for Noverre (*Les petits riens*) and a new symphony (the 'Paris', K. 297 in D) were performed at the Concert Spirituel: the symphony especially was a great success after a nerve-rackingly bad rehearsal, and Wolfgang celebrated afterwards with an ice-cream at the Palais Royal. It was the most mature of his symphonies so far, and it shows how quickly he could assimilate aspects of national style, such as in the brilliant arpeggio passage which opens it – the famous 'premier coup d'archet' (opening bow stroke) of which the French were particularly proud.

But then disaster struck. On 3 July Wolfgang wrote to Leopold that his mother was very ill with a fever, and that all the normal remedies,

ABOVE *The Chapel at Versailles; painting by Jacques Rigaud.*

including those suggested by Baron Grimm's personal physician, had had no effect. He was, in fact, trying to break the terrible news gently to his father. Frau Mozart had died the previous evening. Afraid to tell Leopold the truth, Wolfgang wrote to a family friend, the Abbé Bullinger, asking him to inform his father of his wife's death. Though greatly distressed, Leopold was still concerned about Wolfgang's progress in Paris. He wrote urging him to compose 'something short, easy and popular' which would be suitable for publication. 'How else are you going to live now your pupils are out of town?' asked Leopold. At the same time, Wolfgang (still dreaming about marriage to Aloysia) tactlessly wrote back commending his beloved to Leopold, and asking for his help in establishing Aloysia's career. At the end of August he received another letter from Leopold telling him that the archbishop had forgiven him and wanted a reconciliation. Clearly Leopold had been interceding on Wolfgang's behalf, in the hope of getting him home and back under his jurisdiction as soon as possible. The archbishop was offering Wolfgang his former post as konzertmeister, together with that of court organist, at a substantially increased salary of 500 florins a year, plus the opportunity of leave whenever he needed it to write operas elsewhere. Wolfgang had no choice but to accept such generous terms, and, besides, he was missing his father and sister. He had been away nearly a year, had lost his mother, and was glad to leave Paris ('which I loathe').

The journey home was long and miserable. Baron Grimm, with whom Mozart had finally fallen out, arranged for his departure on a slow, cheap coach, which took 10 days to reach Strasbourg. Unknown to Leopold, Wolfgang intended to travel home via Mannheim, where he hoped to be reunited with Aloysia. But another bitter disappointment awaited him. Circumstances had greatly changed: the Elector Palatine had become also Elector of Bavaria the previous year, and had removed himself and his court – including the orchestra and singers, the Weber family too – to Munich. By this time, Wolfgang had changed his mind about going home. 'The archbishop cannot compensate me enough for slavery in Salzburg . . . I might decide to thumb my nose at him', he wrote. Leopold, having worked so hard to get his son reinstated, was naturally incensed. 'I shall lose my reason, or die of a decline. You must leave *immediately*, or I shall write to Madame Cannabich. God willing, I should like a few more years in which to settle my own account. Then, if you want, you can run wild . . .'

But Wolfgang was set on going to Munich, armed with two new arias for Aloysia. She, however, had changed her mind in the interim, and received him coldly. She later confessed that she had seen in him not a budding genius, but only a 'little man'. Wolfgang bore the blow courageously. After presenting a set of newly engraved sonatas to the elector, he saw that Munich held no further attractions for him. He arrived home on 16 January 1779, just before his 23rd birthday.

Aloysia made her debut in Vienna the same year, and in 1780 she married the court actor and painter Joseph Lange. The marriage was far from happy. Mozart, whose feelings for her took a long time to cool, later wrote more music for her, including the role of Madame Herz in his Singspiel *Der Schauspieldirektor* (The Impresario), and she was the first Viennese Donna Anna in *Don Giovanni*. But the Weber family was destined to play an even more important part in Mozart's future life.

TOP *Aloysia Weber, Mozart's first love, with the man she eventually married, Joseph Lange.*

ABOVE *The Palais Royal, Paris; painting by Jean Lespinasse.*

VI
Idomeneo

As he had done after his return from Italy, Wolfgang settled down once more to life in Salzburg, mitigating the tedium of his official duties – albeit on improved terms – at the archbishop's court with a clutch of compositions. In his next symphony, No 32 in G, K.318, he reverted to the old Italian *sinfonia* form – a shorter, single-movement piece consisting of a slow section sandwiched between two allegros. Two more symphonies followed, both in three movements rather than the traditional four, though Mozart later added a minuet to No.33 in B flat. Around the same time he composed the last of his Salzburg serenades – a brilliant D major piece using a *concertante* group of wind instruments rather than the usual violin, and incorporating a posthorn into one of the minuets – hence its nickname, the 'Posthorn' Serenade.

His contact with French style left its mark particularly in two substantial double concertos (both in E flat), written shortly after his return. Still interested in the sinfonia concertante, he turned his attention to a double piano concerto – K.365 – possibly written for himself and his sister, and one of his first real masterpieces, the Sinfonia Concertante for violin and viola (a medium already used successfully by the Mannheim composer Carl Stamitz). Mozart's work is exquisitely crafted: the instruments seem to engage in a continuous dialogue by turns thoughtful and considered, passionately enraptured (as in the hauntingly beautiful C minor slow movement), and – in the rondo finale – playful, each soloist spurring the other on to more daring feats of imitation.

Several sacred works date from this time: the so-called 'Coronation' Mass, K.317, written for the crowning of a statue of the Virgin Mary in a local church; another *missa brevis* for Salzburg; and two sets of Vespers in six movements (*Vesperae de Domenica*, K.321, and *Vesperae solennes de confessore*, K.339). But the thing he most lacked in Salzburg was the scope to exercise his powers as composer of opera, the genre which interested him the most. In 1779 he began work on a German Singspiel, *Zaïde*, to a text by his father's old friend, Herr Schachtner.

For some reason the piece was never finished or performed, but the extant music bears witness to Mozart's increasingly masterly command of musical characterization, particularly in the ensembles. He also wrote some incidental theatre music for a play by Gebler, *Thamos, König in Ägypten* (Thamos, King of Egypt), which, however, did not remain long in the repertory.

In the summer of 1780 came the long-awaited summons. Despite Mozart's unkind comments on the failing vocal powers of the ageing Mannheim tenor Raaff, some instinct had warned him to keep on friendly terms with the singer, for whom he had written an aria on the way back from Paris. It seems that Raaff's influence with the elector helped to procure Mozart's most important commission to date – an opera to be performed during the 1781 Munich carnival season. The librettist was a Salzburg poet named Varesco, and the work was to be an old-fashioned *opera seria*, following a time-honoured structural formula. The chosen subject came from Greek mythology, though the theme crops up in other myths, including the biblical story of Jeptha. King Idomeneus of Crete, caught in a storm at sea on his way home, vows to Neptune that if he is spared he will sacrifice to the gods the first person he meets on landing – which turns out to be, of course, his own son, Idamantes. The story revolves around the terrible conflict between love and duty as Idomeneus tries desperately to wriggle out of his rash vow, with further complications caused by Idamantes' love for a foreign princess, Ilia, and the relentless pursuit of Idamantes by a singularly determined Cretan lady named Electra.

Mozart began work on the music during the autumn of 1780, and in November the archbishop somewhat grudgingly released him to complete the work in Munich. There he could work closely with the singers, the designer Lorenzo Quaglio, and the ballet-master Pierre Le Grand. The singers included two members of the Wendling family,

LEFT *Anton Raaff, the celebrated tenor who sang the title role in Mozart's* Idomeneo *in Munich in 1781.*

LEFT *One of the original sets for* Idomeneo, *showing the Temple of Neptune, by Lorenzo Quaglio.*

Dorothea and Elisabeth, whom Mozart knew well; Idomeneus was sung by the 66-year-old Raaff, whose voice and acting ability were causing severe problems, while the role of Idamantes was taken by an even worse castrato, Vincenzo dal Prato. Wolfgang's letters to Leopold during the period of composition and rehearsal are full of the problems he encountered: Varesco's libretto was far too long and needed severe pruning; many arias had to be adapted or rewritten to accommodate the foibles of individual singers, and, to make matters worse, Wolfgang himself was suffering from a heavy cold. Finally, the première had to be postponed owing to the sudden death of Empress Maria Theresia. Nevertheless, the opera was finally performed on 29 January 1781, enjoying a triumphant reception, and Wolfgang had the pleasure of being joined for the occasion by Leopold and Nannerl.

Idomeneo, Mozart's first mature opera, is a landmark in the history of opera and one of the few 18th-century *opere serie* to still have regular performances two centuries later; it is also a taste of things to come. Mozart had brought fresh impetus to a time-worn formula thanks to his recent exposure to exciting new developments in Paris. Thus the chorus – often relegated to a small or virtually non-existent role in similar Italian operas, comes to the fore as an integral part of the action, lending real drama and vitality to scenes such as the appearance of the avenging sea monster. Here, for the first time, Mozart demonstrated to the full his superlative skill in making music a medium for the expression of human emotions – in such highlights as Ilia's aria 'Padre, germani, addio', which expresses her conflict between love for her enemy and duty to her native country; Idomeneus' aria 'Fuor del mar', in which the king describes how, although he is physically safe, his mind is still storm-tossed by dark forebodings; and the masterly quartet 'Andrò rammingo e solo' – one of the great operatic ensembles of all time – in which four characters all express different emotions. The ability to convey each individual's feelings within a unified musical number was one of Mozart's unique gifts, and one he was to develop to even greater heights in his later operas.

RIGHT *The Mozart family at the time of* Idomeneo; *painting by Johann Nepomuk della Croce, 1780/1.*

VII
The Breakthrough

Sᴛɪʟʟ ʙᴀsᴋɪɴɢ in the glow of success, Wolfgang and his family took advantage of their employer's absence to relax and enjoy the carnival festivities in Munich. Several new works date from this visit: an oboe quartet for his friend Ramm, some songs, and three piano sonatas, of which K.331 in A contains the famous *Rondo alla turca*. But on 12 March a peremptory summons came from the archbishop, who had gone to Vienna to attend the celebrations marking the accession of the new emperor, Joseph II. Mozart was ordered to join him in Vienna immediately. There he was forcibly reminded of the humiliation of his situation. He, who had been fêted in Munich, had talked with the elector and other noblemen, and been treated with the respect due to a great artist, now had to take his place in the archiepiscopal pecking-order – below the valets, and only slightly higher than the cooks. He was obliged to eat with the servants, and was completely at the archbishop's beck and call. Not surprisingly, the rebellious streak in his nature surfaced, and he started to behave with studied rudeness. Colloredo responded by refusing him permission to play at concerts, and by insisting on his presence at wearisome musical soirées at the archbishop's residence. Mozart was particularly angered when on one particular occasion he was prevented from playing to the emperor and was thereby deprived of a fee equal to half his annual salary.

The situation was clearly reaching boiling point. It finally erupted when Mozart asked for permission to stay on for a few days in Vienna to collect some outstanding fees. Colloredo refused, and, after an abusive interview in which the archbishop lost both his temper and his priestly dignity, calling Mozart a scoundrel and a knave, both parties announced that each was well rid of the other. Colloredo then had second thoughts – Mozart was, after all, quite an asset – and declined to accept his letter of resignation. A misguided attempt to mediate by one of the archbishop's personnel, one Count Arco, led to Mozart's celebrated exit from Colloredo's service with a box on the ear and a boot on the backside.

OPPOSITE *The Emperor Joseph* II (1741–90).

56

'Don't worry about me', wrote Wolfgang to his father. 'I am so certain of my place here that I would have resigned anyway, and now I have good reason three times over . . . my nerve had already failed twice, and couldn't do so again . . .' Leopold was appalled. Once again his son was, it appeared, acting totally irresponsibly, resigning his only secure job with no visible means of support. Quite apart from this impulsive folly, there was another reason for Leopold to be anxious: Wolfgang had written that on being turfed out of the archbishop's

ABOVE *St Stephen's Cathedral, Vienna, where Mozart and Constanze were married.*

lodgings he had taken refuge with his friends the Webers, who had left Munich for Vienna in 1779 when Aloysia was taken on at the German opera. Leopold believed the entire Weber family to be good-for-nothing. He knew that Wolfgang's old affection for Aloysia was not quite dead (even though she was now married), and indeed Wolfgang had recently confessed as much – he truly had loved her, and even now she was not a matter of indifference to him. Fortunately, her jealous 'fool of a husband' kept her under close scrutiny, and Wolfgang was not able to see her often. Aloysia's father had died and Leopold (rightly as it turned out) suspected the motives of his match-making widow. In a private postscript added surreptitiously to one of Wolfgang's letters home from Paris, Frau Mozart had also expressed her anxieties about her son's infatuation with the Webers; as soon as Wolfgang met someone new, he seemed at once ready to dedicate himself to them body and soul, without thinking of his own interests. Leopold accordingly wrote in the sternest terms, castigating his son for leaving the archbishop's service so abruptly, and accusing him (as usual) for thoughtlessness and selfishness. Wolfgang replied in tones of injured innocence, but his father's influence was waning. He had already taken a major decision: he would stay in Vienna.

And within a couple of months, Leopold's fears on one score were proving justified. Madame Weber had clearly decided that this brilliant, if not particularly wealthy, young man would make an admirable son-in-law. Having failed to mate him with Aloysia, she would try another of her daughters.

One of them was the 19-year-old Constanze, six years Mozart's junior. By 20 July Wolfgang was writing to Leopold that he had been obliged to move out of the Weber's house and find different lodgings, since 'people were gossiping'. Rumours were spreading that Mozart was to marry Constanze. Nothing could be further from his mind, he assured Leopold. 'God has not bestowed talent on me for me to dance attendance on a woman, and thereby waste my youth . . .' Besides, he added self-righteously, love didn't come into it: his relations with Constanze were purely platonic.

Mozart indeed had other things on his mind. He had to set about making a living as a free-lance musician. He acquired a few pupils, including an ugly girl named Josepha von Auernhammer, who promptly fell in love with him. She was a talented pianist, but Mozart found it difficult not to show repulsion at his fat, perspiring, scantily clad pupil. 'The sight is enough to strike you blind', he wrote in disgust. Despite his physical antipathy, Mozart wrote a sonata for two pianos (rather than a duet sonata for one keyboard!) for himself and Josepha to play, and dedicated to her a set of six sonatas for piano and violin which was published by the prestigious Viennese firm of Artaria in November, 1781. These are not violin sonatas as we know them, rather sonatas for piano with violin accompaniment.

As well as his teaching, and a planned series of concerts in the autumn, Mozart was also working on a new opera. A Russian grand duke was due to visit Vienna in September, and Mozart had been asked to write a German opera for the occasion. The libretto, by Gottlieb Stephanie, was on a Turkish subject, highly popular in Vienna at the time: the war with Turkey meant that 'Turkish' customs and themes were very much on everyone's minds. It was entitled *Belmont und Constanze*, or *Die Entführung aus dem Serail* (The Abduction from the Harem), and Mozart wrote that he intended to use a 'Turkish' style of music for the overture, for the chorus in Act I and for the closing chorus. (This so-called 'Janissary' style, which Beethoven was to use to such startling effect in the finale of his Ninth Symphony, had already crept into Mozart's music, in the *Rondo alla turca* and the 'Turkish' episode in the finale of the Violin Concerto in A major.) However, it quickly became clear that the opera would not be ready in time for September, even though Mozart had finished the first act by 22 August.

ABOVE A *scene from* Die Entführung; *Mozart's opera was premiered in Vienna in July 1782.*

Just before Christmas, after all his protestations of disinterested friendship with Constanze Weber, Wolfgang now announced to his father that they were to marry. This, according to Wolfgang, would have distinct advantages: it would provide him with a legal outlet for the 'voice of nature', which he swore he had never yet indulged, being too honourable either to seduce innocent girls or have dealings with prostitutes; and a wife would be able to tend his domestic needs – he admitted he was no good at looking after himself. Then, of course, two could live as cheaply as one. True to form, Wolfgang went on to denigrate the entire Weber household except his beloved: Josepha was worthless, fat and a liar; Aloysia insincere, bad-tempered and a flirt; Sophie (the youngest) 'feather-headed'. Constanze, on the other hand was an angel of virtue – the best-hearted and the cleverest. She was not a beauty, it had to be said, but she had a good figure, enough sense to make a good wife and mother, was practical and kind-natured. He ended this eulogy by asking Leopold's blessing on the marriage.

Unknown to him Leopold had recently heard from another composer, Peter von Winter, who had crossed swords with Wolfgang in Mannheim, and was now maliciously taking his revenge. Von Winter had encouraged rumours about Wolfgang and Constanze, implying that the girl had already been seduced. Constanze's guardian accordingly drew up a document that Mozart was required to sign, promising to marry her within three years, or else pay a large sum as compensation. If he refused to sign, he was never to see Constanze again. Wolfgang fell into the trap and signed the document, whereupon Constanze dramatically tore it up, saying that she trusted him and needed no written assurance of his intentions.

All Leopold's correspondence with his son during his engagement was later destroyed by Constanze, so we can only imagine the bitter accusations which must have passed back and forth between Salzburg and Vienna. Even Nannerl was distressed by Wolfgang's new attachment, and complained that he neglected to write to her and her father. Wolfgang replied indignantly that he had no time to write because he was so busy: he got up at six, had his hair dressed, and then composed until nine, after which he gave lessons until lunchtime. He was usually invited out to lunch, resumed work or attended a concert in the evening, and then went to see Constanze, when her mother (who was often drunk) berated both of them. On Sundays he went to the home of Baron van Swieten, an enthusiastic patron of the arts, whose passionate interest in the then neglected music of Bach and Handel stimulated Mozart to collect and study the fugues and other contrapuntal music of J S Bach – an influence which can be detected in his own music of that period. (Rather typically, Mozart ascribed his interest in Bach's music to Constanze's influence; she had 'fallen in love' with fugues, and insisted that Wolfgang should write some of his own.)

OPPOSITE *The title page of an early vocal score of* Die Entführung.

In fact, although Constanze was not such an accomplished singer as her two elder sisters, she was by no means musically illiterate. She too had a good soprano voice, and played the piano reasonably well. There is no reason to suppose that she and Mozart did not discuss his work together, and that he sometimes took her advice. She did, however, give him occasional cause for jealousy: a lover's tiff nearly broke their engagement when Constanze indiscreetly confessed that during a game she had let another young man measure her calves.

During the first half of 1782, Wolfgang continued to work on *Die Entführung*, whose heroine, by coincidence, is also called Constanze. The opera was finally performed in July, and despite some organized opposition, it was a great success. The emperor attended the première, and seemed to approve, despite his observation that it had too many notes ('Just as many as are necessary, your majesty,' Mozart is said to have replied). It had over 20 performances in Vienna alone, and brought Mozart 1,200 florins in the first two days.

Die Entführung (also known as The Seraglio) takes place in a Turkish harem, and concerns the efforts of Belmonte, a Spanish nobleman, to rescue his beloved Constanze, who has been captured by pirates and sold to the Pasha Selim along with her English maid, Blondchen, and Belmonte's servant, Pedrillo (who are, naturally, also in love with each other). The lovers' attempts to escape are frustrated, but the opera ends happily since the Pasha decides that magnanimity is the best course and releases all of them.

Die Entführung is unlike any previous Singspiel, in that it represents a fusion of the technical resources of Italian *opera seria* with the homely tunefulness of the Singspiel. Mozart radically altered the structure of the opera while he was writing it: in a letter to his father he explained how he reconstructed the part of Osmin, the Pasha's Moorish servant

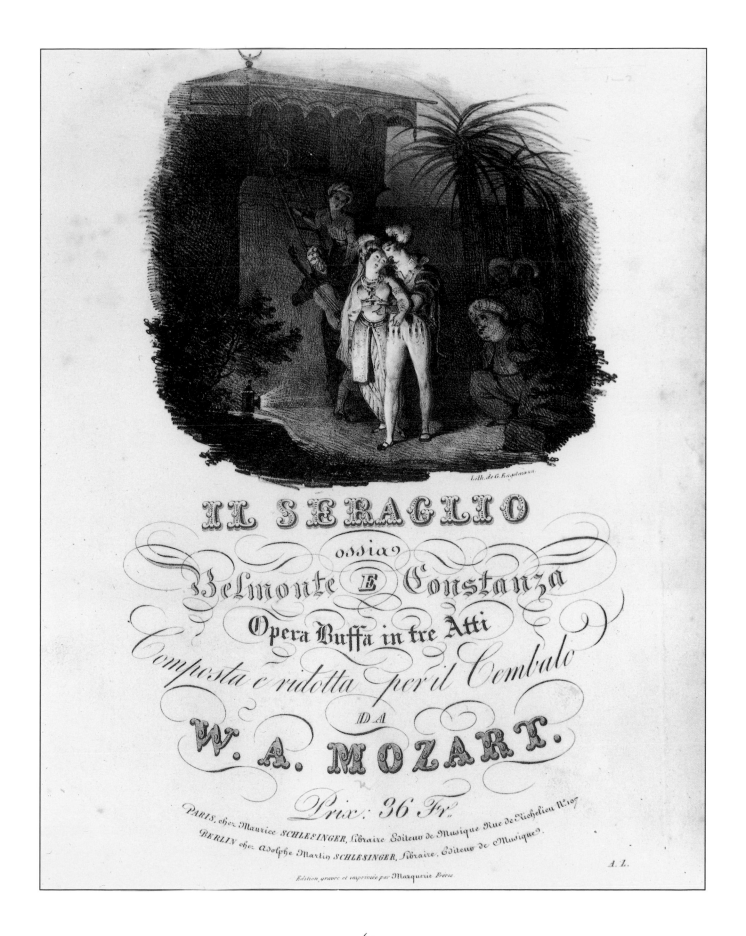

(a negligible role in the original libretto) in order to show off the magnificent bass voice of the singer, Karl Ludwig Fischer, and how the part of Constanze was developed to accommodate the 'flexible throat' of the brilliant Italian coloratura soprano Caterina Cavalieri. *Die Entführung* anticipates the three great *opere buffe* (*Figaro, Don Giovanni* and *Così fan tutte*) in its organic construction, while the 'Turkish' episodes such as the closing Janissary chorus (given Oriental colouring by the use of exotic instruments such as piccolo, triangle, cymbals and bass drum), were 'all that was needed', according to Mozart, to please the Viennese. After *Die Entführung,* the Singspiel was never to be the same again. In 1787 Goethe (then artistic director of the Weimar theatre, and author of a few similar plays) remarked ruefully that *Die Entführung* had put paid to all his efforts to keep the Singspiel simple and modest.

A few days after the première, Constanze's mother decided that matters had gone on long enough between Mozart and Constanze, who had abandoned the fraught atmosphere of home to take temporary refuge with Mozart's friend and patroness, the Baroness von Wald-städten. Frau Weber announced that she would have her daughter returned by the police. Mozart's hand was forced. He decided to wait no longer for his father's permission (which technically he did not need, being over 21). On 27 and 31 July he made two final appeals to Leopold, who had responded curtly to his son's enthusiastic descriptions of his recent musical success; and on 4 August the lovers were married at St Stephen's Cathedral, with only Constanze's mother, her younger sister, her guardian, and two other witnesses present. Leopold's grudging blessing arrived by post the next day. Baroness Waldstädten provided the pair with a 'princely' wedding supper.

Within a couple of months Constanze was pregnant, and Mozart realized that he would soon have a family to support on what was still a precarious income. So far, his hopes for a court position had come to nothing, but his reputation as a pianist and teacher was growing, and his subscription concert series (given in the Burgtheater during Advent and Lent while the theatre was closed for operatic performances) were fairly lucrative. In the early 1780s Viennese society had not yet been drained of financial resources by the long and debilitating war against the Turks, and every aristocrat of note supported some kind of musical establishment, offering a performer such as Mozart plenty of opportunity to give concerts and play at salons.

From Mozart's first year in Vienna date a number of important compositions – the 'Haffner' Symphony, written for a member of the same Salzburg family as the earlier serenade, and itself originally designed as a serenade in brilliant, ceremonial style; the three great wind seren-ades, K.361 in B flat, K.375 in E flat, and K.388 in C minor, each a perfectly crafted gem; the first of a set of six string quartets ultimately completed and published in 1785 as the six 'Haydn' Quartets, dedicated to Joseph Haydn; a group of three piano concertos, K.413 in F, K.414 in A and K.415 in C: and the C minor Mass. This last work was never finished: Mozart seems to have written it as an act of thanksgiving for his marriage, intending Constanze herself to sing as soprano soloist. (Many of the pieces Mozart wrote for his wife, including another set of piano and violin sonatas, remained unfinished, and some biographers have interpreted this as a symptom of Mozart's early disillusionment with his marriage. The truth, more probably, is that he laid them aside to take on commissions for which he would be paid: at this stage in his life he could not afford to compose for sheer pleasure.) The Mass is notable for its assimilation of Baroque contrapuntal elements – further evidence of Mozart's recent preoccupation with Bach and Handel.

The three piano concertos, which Mozart described as a happy medium between what is too easy and what is too difficult – virtuosic, pleasant to listen to, and natural without being banal – were written for himself to play at his subscription concerts. On 29 March he wrote to his father describing the programme at one of these concerts, given in the presence of the emperor. It contained 10 items, including the 'Haffner' Symphony; the aria 'Se il padre perdei' from *Idomeneo,* sung by Aloysia Lange; the new Piano Concerto in C, K.415, played by Mozart himself, together with assorted bits from serenades, arias, and the early Piano Concerto in D, his first genuine concerto with a new rondo finale added. This last was clearly a great hit, as Mozart calls it 'the favourite concerto'. At the end he played a couple of sets of variations as an encore.

Wolfgang's growing success had enabled him and Constanze to move in January 1783 into a new apartment on the Hohenbrücke, on the third floor of No 412. It had a long, narrow study, a bedroom, an antechamber, and a big kitchen, and there was enough room for them to hold a private New Year's ball. There, on 17 June, Constanze gave birth to her first child, a boy, named Raimund Leopold in honour of his godfather, Baron Raimund Wezlar, and his grandfather. During her labour, Wolfgang calmed his nerves by composing the minuet of another string quartet of the 'Haydn' set in D minor. Constanze said many years later that it was an accurate portrayal of her anguish. Only six weeks after her confinement, the Mozarts set out for Salzburg to visit Leopold, a visit promised ever since their marriage but continually put off, much to Leopold's annoyance. They left their newborn baby behind with a wet-nurse, and by 19 August he was dead.

We do not know how Leopold received his daughter-in-law, but the atmosphere must have been strained, to say the least. Wolfgang and Constanze stayed three months, returning to Vienna in the autumn via Linz, where Mozart dashed off a new symphony (K.425 in C, since known as the 'Linz') in record time for concert there. It is his first symphony with a slow introduction – a feature often used by Haydn.

ABOVE *Mozart rehearsing with the soprano Caterina Cavalieri, who first played the role of Constanze in Die Entführung.*

OPPOSITE *Mozart at the keyboard; an unfinished portrait by his brother-in-law Joseph Lange, 1782/3.*

Nor had he been idle in Salzburg: he had written two duos for violin and viola to help out his fellow-composer Michael Haydn, who was in the service of the archbishop. Haydn was ill and could not complete his commission in time, so Mozart finished it for him. Two movements of the Mass in C minor were also given their first hearing in Salzburg cathedral, probably with Constanze singing the soprano part.

The next year of Mozart's life, 1784, was to be his happiest and most successful. His marriage provided sexual fulfilment and domestic peace, marred only by the death of little Raimund Leopold and a chronic shortage of cash. While not exactly extravagant, the couple felt it necessary to establish their place in Viennese society by entertaining their friends in lavish style. Their circle of acquaintances included the cheesemonger and horn-player Ignaz Leutgeb (for whom Mozart wrote four concertos between 1783 and 1791, spattered with jocular comments on Leutgeb's technical shortcomings – 'Bravo!' and 'Oh, you donkey!'); Gottfried von Jacquin, son of the famous botanist Baron von Jacquin and a pupil of Mozart's, for whom Mozart wrote several *notturnos* and some vocal pieces: and a group of expatriate English and Irish musicians. These included Thomas Attwood, a young English composer who took lessons with Mozart, an Irish tenor, Michael Kelly, who sang for four years at the imperial theatre, and became Mozart's favourite billiards partner and drinking companion; another composer, Stephen Storace, who had had two light operas produced in Vienna, and his sister Nancy (Anna), who was principal soprano at the imperial theatre. The charming, vivacious Nancy was to be the

OPPOSITE Thomas Attwood (1765–1838) – organist, composer and conductor – studied with Mozart for two years before returning to England in 1787.

BELOW Mozart wrote his symphony K.425 in C in Linz during a brief stay in 1783.

first Susanna in *The Marriage of Figaro* and Mozart evidently felt a very special affection for her. When she returned to London in 1787 he wrote a brilliant concert aria, 'Ch'io mi scordi di te,' with piano obbligato, for her and himself to play. There is no evidence, however, that she and Mozart were ever lovers, as has been suggested.

Mozart now had a busy teaching and concert schedule. During a five-week period in Lent he gave 19 concerts, some at the homes of aristocrats such as Count Johann Esterházy and the Russian Ambassador, Prince Golitsin, and some privately organized by himself. But he still managed to find time to compose, and in February 1784 he began to keep a catalogue of his music, in which each piece is entered by date. The first entry is the Piano Concerto in E flat, K.449, one of a group of six 'concertos to make you sweat'. K.449 was actually written for one of his pupils, Barbara Ployer, but the next two, K.450 in B flat and K.451 in D, were written for himself. These works mark the beginning of a new maturity in Mozart's style, both in scoring (he now made full use of the range of instruments and good players available in Vienna) and in scope. From now on wind instruments play an increasingly important role, engaging in independent dialogue rather than acting as 'fillers' for the strings. All the orchestral music from 1784 onwards is conceived in broader strokes, while the solo parts become ever more complex.

The next two concertos were written respectively for Barbara Ployer (the intimate, engaging K.453 in G major) and for the blind virtuoso Maria Theresia von Paradis. Viennese by birth, she toured Europe playing and composing in a specially devised, pre-Braille music notation. For her Mozart wrote the powerful concerto K.456 in B flat with its 'hunting-type' finale. Another visiting soloist, the Italian violinist Regina Strinasacchi, inspired a substantial violin sonata, also in B flat (K.454), which soloist and composer played together at a concert. It was written in such haste that only the violin part was copied out for the performance; Mozart played his part from memory. The other major work from this year was the Quintet for piano and wind – 'the best work I have written,' according to Mozart's catalogue.

A further source of joy for Wolfgang and Constanze was the birth of another son in September 1784, christened Carl Thomas. He survived the perils of infancy to live to the ripe old age of 74, but sadly he inherited none of his father's musical talent.

ABOVE *Nancy (Anna) Storace (1765–1817), the soprano for whom Mozart wrote* Ch'io mi scordi di te. *She was also the first Susanna in* The Marriage of Figaro.

OPPOSITE *Mozart's two surviving children, Carl (1784–1858) and Franz Xaver (1791–1844); painting by Hans Hansen, c1798.*

VIII
'The greatest composer known to me'

IN DECEMBER 1784 Mozart became a Freemason. This powerful movement, whose origins are ancient and obscure but which in its modern
form can be said to date from the foundation of the Grand Lodge of
England in 1717, was soon associated with the spread of Enlightenment
ideals through Europe: its ranks included princes, aristocrats, diplomats,
merchants, bankers and civil servants – free-thinkers and rationalists
of the upper and middle classes – as well as intellectuals and artists. By
the mid-century Freemasonry was strong in Austria and Bohemia, but
in the 1780s its activities had come under close scrutiny from the new
emperor, Joseph II, and the Austrian secret police. Perhaps they were
disturbed by alarming reports from France, where the noble philosophical aims of Liberty, Equality and Fraternity were beginning to be
taken a little too far. When Mozart joined the movement many small
lodges were still flourishing in Vienna. He was initiated into the lodge
Zur Wohlthätigkeit (Beneficence) whose Master, the palatine chamberlain Otto von Gemmingen-Homberg, was an old family friend and
patron. In December 1785 Joseph II issued an imperial decree limiting
the number of Viennese lodges to three. Mozart's lodge, with others,
was subsumed into a larger one, Zur neugekrönten Hoffnung (New
Crowned Hope), by which time he had been raised to the third degree,
that of Master Mason. The Master of this new lodge was none other
than the imperial royal chamberlain, Johann, Count Esterházy; while
the Master of Ceremonies was Haydn's employer, Prince Nikolaus
Esterházy. (Haydn joined the Freemasons at the same time as Mozart
though in a different lodge.)

Mozart's involvement with Freemasonry was to have enormous influence on the last seven years of his life. Not only did he write music for
various Masonic ceremonies (such as the *Maurerische Trauermusik*
(Masonic Funeral Music), K.477, for the memorial service of two
fellow-Masons; but, as we shall see, he actually wrote a 'Masonic'
opera that was riddled with the arcane symbolism of the craft – an
incredibly daring act for the member of a society dedicated to absolute

secrecy to do (all its members had to swear an oath to 'hear and conceal' on pain of having their throats cut or their tongues pulled out). Mozart increasingly found himself in need of fraternal charity: as his personal financial situation worsened over the next few years, he was obliged to turn to his brother-Masons for loans (which, to their credit, were almost always forthcoming).

Meanwhile, Mozart's career was at its height. In the spring of 1785 Leopold Mozart paid his son a visit lasting 10 weeks. In a letter to Nannerl (by then married and living in St Gilgen) he wrote in wide-eyed appreciation of Wolfgang's fine apartment 'with all the right furniture' – the Mozarts had moved the previous autumn to a fashionable address in the Schulerstrasse – and he attended a series of six of his son's Lenten subscription concerts. 'Many members of the aristocracy were there, he told Nannerl; 'the concert was magnificent, and the orchestra played excellently.' For these concerts, Wolfgang had written two new piano concertos, which are among his finest. These are K.466

BELOW A *meeting of Mozart's Masonic Lodge in Vienna; anonymous painting.*

in D minor, a passionate, turbulent work of great emotional intensity and spacious proportions; and K.467 in C major, more serene but no less inspired. Both works have slow movements of exquisite and radiant beauty (that of K.467 was used to memorable effect in the film *Elvira Madigan*).

For once in his life, Leopold must have been truly happy: his hopes and prayers for his beloved son seemed at last to have come to fruition. Then, the following Saturday, Joseph Haydn and two aristocratic, musical Masons came to visit Wolfgang. The four of them (Wolfgang on violin), played through Mozart's three new string quartets – the last of the 'Haydn' set. When they had finished, Haydn turned to Leopold and said: 'As God is my witness, and as a man of honour, I tell you that your son is the greatest composer known to me, either personally or by reputation. He has taste and, what is more, the most complete knowledge of composition.'

Leopold must have been overcome with emotion. The next day he attended another concert at which Wolfgang played the 'glorious concerto' written the previous December for Mademoiselle Paradis (K.456 in B flat). Leopold was sitting only two boxes away from the beautiful Princess of Wurttemburg, and he confessed he was so moved by the magical instrumental interplay that, for 'sheer delight', tears sprang to his eyes. When Mozart left the platform, the emperor waved his hat, and shouted 'Bravo, Mozart!'

Leopold was naturally intensely interested in his son's financial affairs, and reported to Nannerl that, if Wolfgang had no debts, he should soon be able to put 2,000 gulden in the bank. So far as the housekeeping was concerned, Leopold had to admit that Constanze was doing a good job, and seemed to be extremely economical. Nevertheless, despite all the money flowing in from concerts, pupils and publications, Mozart was indeed in debt again by the year's end and was having to beg a loan from his publisher Franz Anton Hoffmeister – for whom his next string quartet, K. 499 (the 'Hoffmeister'), was written, perhaps in gratitude. Towards the end of April Leopold returned to Salzburg, well content with his son's achievements. Neither knew that they would never meet again.

On 1 September 1785 Mozart dispatched his six 'Haydn' quartets to their dedicatee, accompanied by a humble and touching letter. In it, he entrusted his 'six sons' to the protection of his 'most celebrated and very dear friend', adding that they were the products of long and laborious labour, but that he was encouraged by the hope that one day they would prove a source of consolation. He entreated Haydn to overlook those faults which may have escaped 'a father's biased eye', and begged him to continue his friendship towards 'one who values it so highly'.

A large quantity of Mozart's music was published in that year, 1785, perhaps reflecting the ever-growing demand from the newly affluent

ABOVE A *silhouette of Mozart by Hieronymus Löschenkohl, 1785.*

OPPOSITE *Joseph Haydn (1732–1809); portrait by Guttenbrunn.*

middle classes for music which they could buy and play at home. Artaria & Co published the six 'Haydn' quartets, of which the last three were K.458 in B flat, known as the 'Hunt' because of its 'hunting-style finale; K.464 in A, and K.465 in C, the remarkable 'Dissonance' Quartet, so-called because of its intensely chromatic slow introduction. As well as these, Artaria also published two symphonies, the 'Haffner' and No 33 in B flat; the three piano concertos K.413–5, and the substantial Fantasia and Sonata in C minor for keyboard. Both through publications and performances, Mozart's fame was spreading rapidly. *Die Entführung* was being performed all over Austria and Germany, and, according to Leopold, the Berlin papers were advertising the new quartets, saying that Mozart's name alone was sufficient to recommend them to the public: no other guarantee of quality was needed.

In the same letter to Nannerl, of 3 or 4 November, 1785, Leopold was grumbling that he hadn't heard a word from Wolfgang recently, but that a journalist friend had mentioned something about a new opera. A week later, the news was out. Wolfgang had begun work on an operatic version of Beaumarchais' controversial play *Le Mariage de Figaro*, which had been performed for the first time in Paris the year before. The plot, which concerned unseemly and immoral behaviour among the upper classes and their humiliation by their servants, was considered too daringly outspoken (and doubtless too uncomfortably near the truth) by those same aristocrats, and a German version had been banned by imperial decree in Vienna early in 1785. Leopold was understandably worried by his son's involvement in a possible political controversy. 'I know the piece', he wrote; 'it is a very silly play and the translation will have to be altered a great deal if it is to work as an opera . . . God grant that the libretto will be successful. For the music, I have no doubts . . .'

Mozart's librettist for *Figaro* was himself a controversial and colourful character. Lorenzo da Ponte (1749–1838), the son of a converted Jewish tanner, started out as an ordained priest, but any hopes of a successful career in that direction were scotched by his uncontrollably amorous nature. He took up writing opera libretti, and came to Vienna around 1780, where he obtained a court appointment. *Figaro* was his first real success, and he and Mozart worked closely on the text, toning down the political comment, and emphasizing the comic (*buffo*) elements so perfectly suited to Mozart's deft, sparkling setting. It was apparently Da Ponte who persuaded the emperor to pass the text, telling him that all scenes which might offend good taste or public decency had been excised.

Just as *Die Entführung* changed the face of the Singspiel, so *The Marriage of Figaro* is a landmark in the history of *opera buffa*. Nothing that preceded it could have prepared its audience for a work of such comic brilliance, masterly characterization, and sheer breadth of conception. Mozart and Da Ponte reduced the original five acts to four,

ABOVE *Lorenzo da Ponte (1749–1838) wrote the libretti for* The Marriage of Figaro, Don Giovanni *and* Cosi fan tutte.

OPPOSITE *Pierre Augustin Caron de Beaumarchais (1732–1799), author of* The Marriage of Figaro; *anonymous portrait.*

but all Beaumarchais' complicated plots and sub-plots are retained. The story is complex. It is a sequel to *The Barber of Seville* by the same author (later to be turned into an opera by Rossini). In that play, the resourceful barber Figaro helped his master Count Almaviva, a young Spanish nobleman, to rescue the lovely Rosina from the clutches of her guardian Doctor Bartolo, who wanted to marry her himself. When *The Marriage of Figaro* begins, the count has been married to Rosina for several years, and is beginning to tire of her. Figaro, now promoted to personal valet, is to marry the countess's vivacious maid Susanna, on whom the count has dishonourable designs. As she is impervious to his suggestions, he is determined to revive the old custom known as the *droit du seigneur* (one of the most hated abuses of the Ancien Régime), whereby the lord of a manor was entitled to deflower his female servants before their weddings. The plot of the opera concerns the efforts of Figaro, Susanna and the countess acting in collusion to frustrate the count's plan. There are, of course, further complications, notably in the form of Cherubino, an adolescent page-boy who is romantically in love with the countess (a feeling which is almost

BELOW The title page of an early vocal score of Figaro.

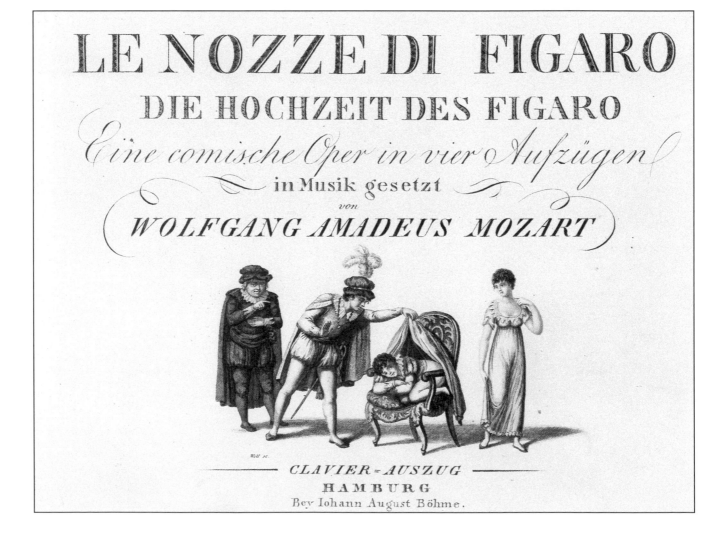

mutual, and to which the count takes exception), and in the fact that Figaro is being pursued by an old harpy named Marcellina, who is trying to trick him into marriage with her. But all ends well: Marcellina turns out to be Figaro's long-lost mother; he and Susanna are safely married; and the humiliated count is (at least temporarily) reconciled with his countess.

Mozart wrote the music in a specific order: first the comic arias, then the action ensembles, and lastly the lyric arias. Each character is musically differentiated: the countess has two magnificently melancholic arias in which she laments the loss of her husband's affection; the count is portrayed as arrogant, cynical and menacing; Figaro and Susanna are quick-witted, likeable, scheming and intelligent, able to give as good as they get, but both capable as well of jealousy and emotional suffering; Cherubino is a confused adolescent who has just discovered sex but doesn't know what to do with it. And minor characters such as Basilio, the oily music-master, Antonio the inebriated gardener, the vengeful Bartolo and Marcellina, and Barbarina, the dumb-blonde go-between, are all equally deftly portrayed.

Mozart's fine understanding of key-schemes enabled him to build-up large-scale musical structures that were closely linked to the fast-moving action. The second and fourth acts end with massive, sectional ensemble finales in which varying numbers of characters appear and disappear, as in a farce, and create new crises (to which solutions rapidly have to be found) that contribute to the overall pace and tension of the drama. The finale of Act Two is an unsurpassed *tour de force* of this kind, lasting 20 minutes without a break. Act One ends with Figaro's celebrated aria 'Non più andrai', which became an instant hit, while Act Three ends with a ballet incorporating a Spanish fandango – the only bit of 'local colour' in the whole opera.

Despite a good deal of organized opposition and intrigue from Mozart's enemies in court circles, of whom the ringleader was probably Antonio Salieri, *Figaro* was first performed in the Burgtheater on 1 May, 1786. The cast included Nancy Storace as Susanna and Michael Kelly as Don Basilio. It was well received at first, and Mozart made 450 gulden out of it. But then, unaccountably, its initial popularity dropped off, and it only had eight further performances that year. Leopold put its relative failure down to conspiracy, saying darkly that 'powerful cabals' had united in opposition to Wolfgang because of jealousy of his exceptional talent.

The composition of *Figaro* occupied Mozart almost exclusively for six months. In early 1786 the governor-general of the Netherlands visited Vienna with his wife, the Archduchess Christine, sister of the emperor. In honour of the occasion, Mozart was to write a short Singspiel, again to a libretto by Gottlieb Stephanie, called *Der Schauspieldirektor* (The Impresario). This, together with a piece by Mozart's rival Salieri, was given in the orangery at the Schönbrunn palace on 7

TOP *Michael Kelly, a friend of Mozart's and the first Don Basilio.*

ABOVE *The Domgasse, Vienna, where Mozart was living when he wrote* Figaro.

77

February: it had taken just two weeks to write. The one-act opera, which concerns the tribulations of an impresario who manages a travelling opera company, was described by the composer as a 'comedy with music'. The cast included Aloysia Lange, and her husband Joseph in a speaking role; Salieri's mistress Caterina Cavalieri, and the author of the text, Stephanie himself, as the eponymous impresario. The sparkling overture is still often played today.

Between December and March, Mozart found the time to write three more piano concertos for his subscription concerts (K.482 in E flat, K.488 in A, and K.491 in C minor). The last two – works of completely contrasting character – were written within a few weeks of each other. K.488 is one of Mozart's sunniest, most straight-forwardly appealing works, with a delightful 'siciliana' slow movement; while K.491 is a richly chromatic, dark-hued piece in which the opening motif supplies material for densely argued thematic development throughout.

Unlike the previous year Mozart only appears to have given one concert during Lent; was he simply too busy, or was he perhaps no longer in quite such demand? Such concerts were probably getting fewer anyway, since former patrons may have found their own financial resources increasingly strained by the exigencies of the continuing war with Turkey. Mozart was clearly concerned about money, and in the summer of 1786 he offered a number of his compositions to the Prince von Fürstenberg, hoping for a fixed annual salary in return. (These included four symphonies, five piano concertos and various chamber works, of which the prince took a selection, but declined to grant the retainer.) In October Mozart's English friends tried to persuade him to join them in England the following spring. Leopold, asked to act as babysitter for his grandchildren Carl and a new baby, Johann, born on 18 October, grumpily declined, and the proposed visit had to be cancelled. Poor little Johann survived less than a month.

Towards the end of the year an important invitation arrived from Prague, the Bohemian capital, which had taken *Figaro* to its heart with unbridled enthusiasm. Mozart and Constanze arrived in the city on 11 January 1787. In a letter to his friend Gottfried von Jacquin Wolfgang described how he attended a ball that evening, at which the cream of Bohemian society, including a bevy of attractive ladies, was present. He looked on 'with the greatest pleasure' while all these people danced to the music of *Figaro*, arranged – according to the custom of the time – as quadrilles and waltzes. The tunes were on everyone's lips: they were played, sung and whistled in the streets; the whole city had gone 'Figaro-mad'.

Mozart thoroughly enjoyed his visit. He attended two performances of *Figaro* and gave a concert at the opera house, which included the première of a new symphony he had written specially (K.504, known afterwards as the 'Prague'). The recently written Piano Concerto in C,

K.503, may also have been intended for performance there, but none is recorded. In Prague, Mozart also reacquainted himself with old friends, including Count Thun, in whose house he and Constanze stayed, and the Dušeks – František, a respected composer and teacher, and his wife Josepha, an old Salzburg friend of Wolfgang's and a fine singer for whom he had written several concert arias.

But the most important outcome of the visit was another opera commission, for production in Prague in the autumn of 1787. On returning to Vienna in February, Mozart immediately asked Da Ponte for a new libretto. The ex-abbé, possibly with tongue-in-cheek considering his own record, suggested the subject of Don Juan, the archetypal libertine, and dropped other projects to begin work immediately.

At the beginning of April that year, Wolfgang heard that his father was dangerously ill. He wrote Leopold a philosophical letter which has since become famous, in which he said that over the past few years he had come to regard death as the 'true goal' of man's existence, and that he had become so closely acquainted with this 'best and truest friend' that the image of death was no longer terrifying, but rather reassuring and consoling. Leopold had joined the Freemasons on his visit to Vienna in 1785, so father and son shared an additional ideological bond. Nonetheless, although Wolfgang ends his letter (dated 4 April) by expressing the desire to come to his dying father's arms 'as soon as is humanly possibly', he did not do so. Leopold died just under two months later, alone, on 28 May. His old friend, the abbot of St Peter's Abbey in Salzburg, noted that Leopold had been a man of 'much wit and wisdom', whose talents went far beyond those of music alone, yet he had 'had the misfortune always to be persecuted' and was consequently held in less esteem in Salzburg than elsewhere in Europe.

Despite their differences and Leopold's difficult and austere character, his father's death robbed Wolfgang of a most loving and tender parent, and of one of the few people who genuinely appreciated and fully comprehended the nature of his genius. Leopold's tragedy was that of a parent whose cherished child spurns his advice in adolescent rebellion; but, unlike, for example, Alessandro Scarlatti, another musician father with a son more brilliant than himself, Leopold could never quite bring himself to untie the emotional leashes and allow his own 'young eagle whose wings are grown' to find his own way in the world.

Wolfgang was undoubtedly genuinely grieved at the loss of his father, but his main preoccupation was with practical matters and the maintenance of his own family. He made over his share in Leopold's estate to Nannerl in return for 1,000 gulden of ready cash, which he desperately needed. In April he and Constanze had moved to a smaller, less fashionable apartment on the Landstrasse, and Constanze was once again pregnant. While working on the new opera, *Don Giovanni*, he also completed two string quintets, K.515 in C and K.516 in G minor

ABOVE A *page from Mozart's autograph manuscript of the C minor Piano Concerto, K.491.*

– one of his greatest works in that key; the Violin Sonata in A, K.526; and two small-scale 'divertimento-style' pieces, the exquisite serenade *Eine Kleine Nachtmusik*, and its antithesis, *Ein musikalischer Späss* (A Musical Joke), which, in its wealth of wrong notes and inept harmonies, is obviously intended to be a satire on incompetent composers. During this time Mozart may have given some lessons to the young Beethoven, who was visiting Vienna for the first time.

On 1 October 1787 Mozart and Constanze again left for Prague, with the incomplete score of *Don Giovanni*. The rest was written in the Dušek's residence, the Villa Bertramka, in a village outside the city; and the new opera was premièred after some delay on 29 October, with huge success. It was only just finished in time: according to Constanze, the overture (the last section to be composed) was completed just two days before the première. Mozart's friends in Prague

tried to persuade him to stay on to write another opera, but he declined. Constanze's next confinement was close and she probably wanted to get home.

Don Giovanni, though technically an *opera buffa*, is far removed from the light-hearted comedy of *Figaro*, in which characters change clothes, hide in cupboards and jump out of windows. It begins with an attempted rape and a murder, contains scenes of spine-chilling horror when the murder victim's marble effigy comes to life in the graveyard and then accepts its murderer's invitation to supper, and ends with the unrepentant libertine being dragged down to hell by demons. The female characters, too, are made of sterner stuff than the quick-witted schemers of *Figaro*. Donna Anna, daughter of the murdered Commendatore, lacks any sense of humour: she is aiming to be a heroine of high drama; while Donna Elvira, one of Giovanni's cast-offs, is a genuinely tragic figure: mocked by all and in danger of losing her reason, she remains touchingly faithful to the lover who has abandoned her. And Mozart provided music to match such emotions. The predominant key of the opera is D minor, a sombre key with overtones of night and death; while the dramatic scenes in the graveyard and at Giovanni's last supper-party, when the statue appears for the last time, are reinforced with funereal-sounding trombones.

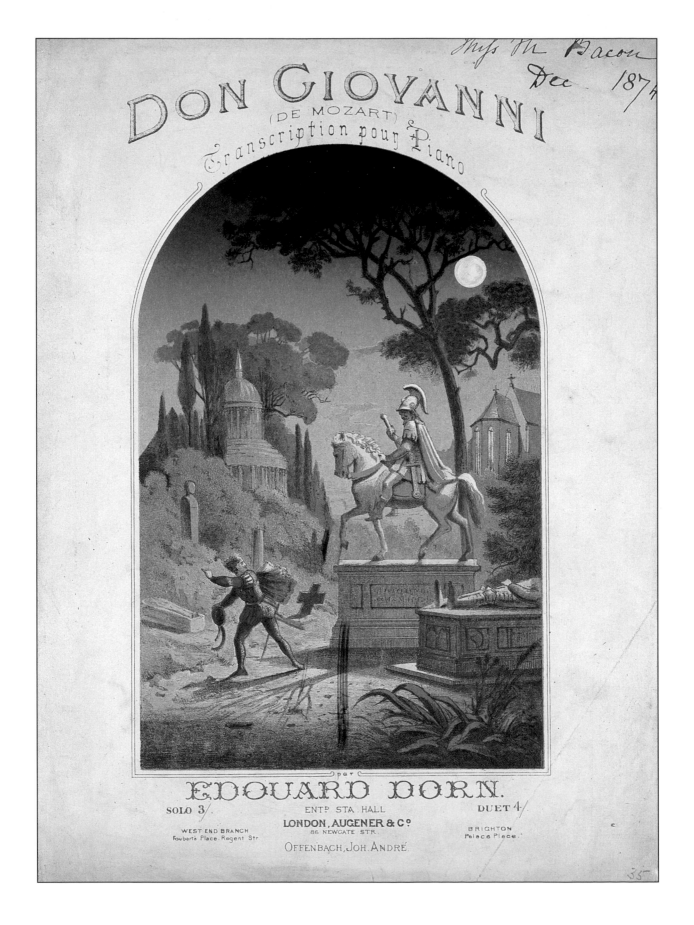

There are, of course, moments of light relief. Giovanni has a comic side-kick, his servant Leporello, whose grumbling aria – he is forced to wait outside while his master amuses himself indoors – opens the opera. It is he who taunts Elvira with the famous 'Catalogue' aria, listing his master's conquests: 640 in Italy, 231 in Germany, 100 in France, 91 in Turkey, and 1,003 (so far) in Spain. Leporello is hiding under the table when Giovanni meets his just desserts; he survives to tell the tale and to join in the final ensemble warning the audience to take heed of the libertine's dreadful fate.

The other *buffo* characters are a peasant couple, Zerlina and Masetto, whose wedding celebrations Giovanni interrupts with his customary rake-hell intentions. It is with Zerlina that Giovanni sings the enchanting duet 'La cì darem la mano', which later composers, including Chopin, paid the compliment of using as the basis for variations. In an opera overflowing with such individual gems as the famous 'Champagne' aria and the charming serenade with mandolin accompaniment 'Deh vieni all' finestra', Mozart still could not resist showing off his technical skill. In the ballroom scene which ends Act One, he writes parts for three separate bands playing different kinds of dance music simultaneously – a minuet for the aristocracy, a contredanse for Giovanni and Zerlina (a couple of mixed social status), and a German dance for the peasants. Similarly, in the finale to Act Two, Giovanni's last supper is accompanied by a wind-band playing excerpts from three well-known contemporary operas – including 'Non più andrai' from Mozart's own *Figaro*!

On his return to Vienna in November 1787, Mozart's fortunes received an unexpected boost – his first permanent appointment at the Viennese court as kammermusicus (chamber composer). Admittedly, the salary was not wonderful (800 gulden per annum, whereas the previous incumbent, Gluck, had been paid 2,000), but the duties were light. All he had to do was provide music for the court balls. On the strength of this extra income, Mozart moved his family to another apartment, Unten den Tuchlauben, where on 27 December 1787 Constanze gave birth to a daughter, Theresia. She lived only six months.

By the time of his little daughter's death in June 1788, Mozart's finances were in a desperate state, and he had begun to write a series of begging letters to his friend and fellow-Mason, Michael Puchberg. Three of these date from June alone, during which month the Mozarts moved again, this time to a cheaper apartment outside the town. At the same time, in a white-hot creative burst, Mozart began work on a group of three symphonies – K.543 in E flat, K.550 in G minor, and K.551 in C (the 'Jupiter').

Until very recently, it was thought that these symphonies, unlike almost all Mozart's other music, were written for no specific occasion, but as the result of an inner impulse. It is now believed that they may

OPPOSITE *An illustrated title page of* Don Giovanni.

ABOVE *The title page of the vocal score of* Don Giovanni.

OPPOSITE *Christoph Willibald von Gluck (1714–87); anonymous portrait. Mozart inherited Gluck's position as chamber composer at the Viennese court following the latter's death.*

BELOW *Mozart; boxwood medallion by Leonard Posch, 1789.*

have been written for a subscription concert series in 1788 – the 'Casino' series mentioned in a letter to Puchberg, which may have taken place in the autumn. Each of the three has a different character, and each is scored for a different combination of instruments. The E flat, which uses clarinets instead of oboes, one flute, and pairs of bassoons, horns, trumpets and drums, is a spacious and serene work of grace and charm; the G minor, which restricts its wind to one flute and pairs of oboes, bassoons and horns (to which Mozart later added clarinets), has a driving, almost tragic urgency, relaxing only in the exquisite slow movement; while the majestic 'Jupiter', the summit of Mozart's symphonic achievement, has an expansive grandeur crowned by a magnificent contrapuntal finale. Clarinets are, however, omitted from its scoring in favour of a pair of oboes. The clarinet, a relatively new instrument, had not been available in Salzburg, but was becoming increasingly common by the 1780s. Mozart, who loved its flexibility and smooth, resonant tone, used it more and more in his later works, especially in those with Masonic connections. Another favourite instrument of his late period is the basset-horn, a relative of the clarinet with a lower range and deeper timbre.

Apart from the symphonies, Mozart's compositions of 1788 include the Piano Concerto in C, K.503, written in February (it is not known if Mozart ever played it in public); several new numbers for the Vienna première of *Don Giovanni* in May (despite starring Caterina Cavalieri as Donna Elvira and Aloysia Lange as Donna Anna, the opera was even less successful there than *Figaro*, having only 15 further performances); three piano trios written for Puchberg; a piano sonata, and a quantity of light vocal music. In order to make a little extra money, the most inventive composer of his time was reduced to making arrangements of earlier music, especially Handel's, for concerts sponsored by Baron van Swieten. To these we owe the 'Mozart versions' of *Acis and Galatea* and *Messiah*.

IX
The End

BY MARCH 1789 Mozart had become accustomed to sending regular letters to his fellow-Masons and publishers asking for loans. One such was sent to Franz Hofdemel, whose young wife Magdalene was a pupil of Mozart's, requesting 100 gulden to finance another trip abroad. Prince Karl Lichnowsky had offered to take Mozart to Berlin, where he would be introduced to King Friedrich Wilhelm II. They set out on 8 April, stopping first at Prague. There a new opera commission was discussed with Domenico Guardasoni, manager of the National Theatre; this may have been an embryonic version of *La clemenza di Tito*, Mozart's last opera, which he was to write for Prague two years later.

Mozart's visit to Berlin is well documented from his frequent letters to his wife, which are full of affectionate concern for her health (she was, of course, pregnant once more), and anxiety for the propriety of her conduct in his absence. 'Do be careful of your honour and mine, and consider appearances', he begged her. Constanze was clearly not ill enough to be incapable of a little mild flirtation!

In Dresden, where he and Lichnowsky stayed for a week, Mozart heard a Mass by the court composer Naumann ('very weak stuff it was') performed at court. There he played his own Piano Concerto in D, K.537, for which he received yet another snuffbox, and heard an organ recital by J. W. Hässler, whose teacher had studied with J. S. Bach. Mozart didn't rate his playing highly. He also attended the opera, which he found 'abominable'.

The next stop was Leipzig, and then Potsdam and the Prussian court. Mozart returned briefly to Leipzig to give another concert, at which he played the Piano Concerto in B flat, K.456, but it brought him little return. By this time he was writing rather apologetically to Constanze, telling her that she must be more delighted to see him back in person than with any money he would be bringing in – he had even been obliged to lend his impecunious patron Prince Lichnowsky 100 gulden, a request he could hardly refuse . . . On 26 May Mozart

ABOVE *Potsdam.*

appeared at court before the King of Prussia, a keen amateur cellist, who may have asked for some quartets. These were the three 'Prussian' quartets, K.575 in D, K.589 in B flat, and K.590 in F, Mozart's last, which he certainly began composing on the way home from Berlin, but did not complete until the following year. He arrived home on 4 June, to a passionate reunion with his wife (if his letters, full of expressions of his desire for her, are to be believed).

By July, however, both Wolfgang and Constanze were ill, and Mozart was once more writing to Puchberg for money, in view of his inability to work. This illness, a recurrence of the same symptoms (violent colic, with spells of vomiting and attacks of fever) that he had suffered intermittently over the past few years, was a sombre presage of his final illness, now only two years away. According to his letter to Puchberg, he had tried to organize a further series of subscription concerts to improve his finances, but when the list came back only the faithful Baron van Swieten's name was on it. The desertion of the fickle Viennese public, who had once flocked to hear him, was a severe blow and Wolfgang was deeply ashamed to have to beg once more from his 'only friend'.

Constanze, then four or five months pregnant, was also in a wretched state, and at one point Mozart feared for her life. She had evidently injured her foot, and they thought the bone might be affected. After

some hesitation the estimable Puchberg responded to Mozart's appeal, and Constanze was dispatched to take a cure at Baden, a spa about 17 miles south of Vienna. She seems to have had amazing powers of recovery: from being at death's door in mid-July, a month later she was giving her husband cause for concern about 'making herself cheap' in the free-and-easy atmosphere of Baden. 'Do not torment yourself and me with needless jealousy', implored Wolfgang. 'Do remember that a wife can only enslave her husband by her modest behaviour.'

Constanze was to spend a good deal of time over the next two years at Baden, where her husband often visited her. Over the summer of 1789, while she was away, he wrote a couple of new arias (including the delightful 'Un moto di gioia') for a new production of *Figaro*, at the request of the Susanna (Adriana Ferraresi del Bene). He also completed the first (and only one) of a projected set of six piano sonatas for the King of Prussia's daughter, and the sublime Clarinet Quintet, K.581, for his friend Anton Stadler – a fine clarinettist, but a distinctly unreliable character. It was first performed at a meeting of the Tonkünstler-Societät in December.

During the autumn Mozart was commissioned by the emperor to write another *opera buffa*, again to a libretto by Da Ponte. This was *Così fan tutte* (roughly translated – They're all the same), one of Mozart's greatest musical achievements, but an opera which remained misunderstood for over 150 years after his death. Beethoven, among others, could not comprehend how Mozart could have stooped so low as to set to music such an apparently frivolous text, dealing with the fickleness of women; and the prudish moral climate of the later 19th century made sure that *Così* was conveniently ignored as a little aberration. The opera, for which Mozart received a fee of 200 ducats, was first performed on 26 January 1790 at the Burgtheater, and had four more performances before the death of Joseph II put a temporary end to all theatrical events in Vienna. Nevertheless, once the period of court mourning was over, *Così* was revived with a reasonable degree of success. Clearly its light-hearted character appealed more to contemporary taste than the complexities – musical and textual – of *Figaro*, or of *Don Giovanni*, with its reminder of the dreadful fate awaiting the over-indulgent sensualist.

Così has six principal characters – two pairs of lovers, a cynical old 'philosopher' named Don Alfonso, and the girls' maid, Despina. The chorus plays a minimal role. The two young men, Guglielmo and

BELOW Baden, where Constanze Mozart spent much of the years 1789–91 for the sake of her health.

Ferrando, are teased by Don Alfonso, who tells them that all women are the same – fundamentally faithless by nature. Naturally the two officers protest that *their* girls are different, but Alfonso persuades them to put it to the test. They arrange to be 'called up' on active service, duly disappear after an emotional farewell, and promptly reappear in disguise as two 'Albanian' merchants. Each woos the other's sweetheart passionately, and after initial indignant reluctance, the girls begin to give way, much to their sweethearts' disgust. Eventually proposals of marriage are made and accepted, but during the ceremony – performed by Despina in disguise as the notary – military sounds are heard and the girls realize with horror that their original sweethearts are 'returning'. Guglielmo and Ferrando reappear without their disguises, and the girls become aware that they have been tricked. Accusations, excuses and explanations ensue, but in the end all is forgiven: it's only the way of the world, according to Don Alfonso. The only question that remains is – who is to marry whom?

The six characters of *Così fan tutte*, appearing in various permutations throughout, provided Mozart with a custom-made vehicle for his skill in deft musical characterization. Thus two of the lovers, Fiordiligi and Ferrando, are more heavyweight characters than the other pair. Ferrando is the least happy with the eventual outcome; his faith in women has been permanently shaken. And Fiordiligi puts up more resistance than her sister Dorabella, and her brilliant coloratura arias reflect her emotional torment. Dorabella's music is lighter in style: she is a charming, fluffy creature, more ready to listen to the siren song of pleasure. The quick-witted Despina is a delightful character, the archetypal soubrette, just like Adèle in *Die Fledermaus*. She spends much of the opera in disguise, first as a 'doctor' who 'revives' the Albanians (who have pretended to kill themselves when rejected) by means of an enormous magnet (thanks to Dr Mesmer), and then as the notary who is to perform the marriage ceremony.

Così is above all an ensemble opera. Act One opens with three trios for the men, followed by a duet for the sisters, and goes on to include two quintets (one of which is the heavenly 'Di scrivermi ogni giorno', during which the lovers bid farewell while Don Alfonso comments cynically in the background, and the exquisitely beautiful trio for the two girls and Don Alfonso, 'Soave sia il vento' (featured in the film *Sunday, Bloody Sunday*). Act Two, during which the wooing gets seriously under way, is naturally more devoted to arias, including Fiordiligi's magnificent rondo 'Per pietà, ben mio', and Ferrando's 'revenge' aria 'Tradito, schernito', and duets for the rearranged couples. The finale includes a cunningly constructed canon during which Ferrando, still heartbroken, at first refuses to take part, until he is gradually drawn in by the others.

Despite the substantial fee which Mozart received for *Così*, he was still deeply in debt. Puchberg continued to respond to his appeals with

ABOVE Mozart in 1789; after a
drawing by Doris Stock.

incredible generosity, but the money went immediately on doctors' bills. (Yet another of Constanze's pregnancies had ended in tragedy: another daughter, Anna, had been born and died the previous November.) In April 1790 Mozart was hoping for another court appointment under the new emperor, Leopold II, and he implored Puchberg to keep his financial disarray a secret, believing that if it were publicly known it would damage his chances of success. He petitioned Leopold II for the post of vice-kapellmeister, emphasizing his own track-record as a composer of sacred music (a field in which Salieri, who had been appointed kapellmeister in 1788, was not particularly proficient), but received no response. In June, he told Puchberg bitterly that he had been forced to give away his 'Prussian' quartets for a song, just in order to have enough cash to meet his present obligations. For some unknown reason their original dedicatee never took them up, and the set was eventually published, without a dedication, after Mozart's death.

After spending part of the summer at Baden with Constanze, Mozart decided to go on speculation to Frankfurt am Main, where Leopold II was to be crowned Holy Roman Emperor on 9 October. Hoping to attract the new emperor's attention, Mozart set off with his brother-in-law, in his own coach, arriving at Frankfurt on 28 September, after a quick, six-day journey. On 15 October he gave an 'academy' (a concert) at the city theatre: the programme included two piano concertos which he played himself (K.459 in F, noted by one listener as a work of 'gentillesse and great charm', and K.537 in D, subsequently known as the 'Coronation'), a symphony (presumably one of the 1788 group), and various arias and piano pieces. The small orchestra was 'feeble', and Mozart wrote sadly to his wife that the concert had been a great success from the point of view of honour and glory, but a complete financial flop. Back in Vienna, Constanze, for once not pregnant, had begun to take over the financial reins with great aplomb. Mozart's letters from Frankfurt are full of references to a mysterious deal that was to be the solution to all their problems. A Viennese merchant, Heinrich Lackenbacher, was to advance Mozart 1,000 florins in cash, at 5 per cent interest, against his furniture as security. Then Mozart would supply the publisher Hoffmeister with a series of compositions which would bring him enough revenue to repay the debt over two years. In Mozart's absence, Constanze organized and concluded the deal. She also arranged their next move, to an apartment in the Rauhensteingasse in the centre of Vienna. It was to be Mozart's last address.

He, meanwhile, was clearly depressed by his lack of success in Frankfurt. He had failed to win the emperor's attention, and his chronic money problems were weighing heavily upon him. 'If anyone could see into my heart, I should feel quite ashamed', he wrote to his wife. 'Everything is cold to me – as cold as ice.' Torn between his longing to be home again, and his ambition to bring back enough money to have made the trip worthwhile, he considered extending his tour to places which had formerly welcomed him, but, in the end, his homesickness proved too much for him, and he left Frankfurt the day after his concert. His homeward journey took him via Mainz, where he gave a concert before the elector; Mannheim, where *Figaro* was being performed; Augsburg, Munich and Linz. He arrived back in Vienna in November, when his sixth and last child was conceived.

A month later, he said his final goodbye to another dear friend – Joseph Haydn. The elder composer, finally released from servitude at

RIGHT *Emmanuel Schikaneder (1751–1812) – actor, singer, writer, producer and the manager of the Theater auf der Wieden – was an old friend of Mozart's and encouraged him in writing* Die Zauberflöte.

Esterháza, had been invited to visit London by the impresario J P Salomon, who also intended to entice Mozart to England. Discussions took place, and Mozart tentatively agreed to follow on the next season. The parting between the two great composers was poignantly prescient. Mozart said goodbye with tears in his eyes, saying, 'I fear that this is the last time we shall ever see each other.' The 58-year-old Haydn took this to mean that Mozart feared that his friend might not survive the long and hazardous journey. He could not have foreseen that it would be Mozart, 24 years his junior, who would be dead before the year's end.

Over the spring of 1791 Mozart busied himself with composition: pieces for mechanical organ (a fashionable instrument he detested); two string quintets, K.593 in D and K.614 in E flat, both written for private concerts at the homes of wealthy amateurs; a great deal of dance music – minuets, German dances, etc. – for the court balls; and a new piano concerto, in B flat, K.595. This, a piece whose mellow, introverted character has led many commentators to see in it the hand of a composer approaching the end of his life, was the work with which Mozart made his last public appearance, in March at a benefit concert for a clarinettist friend. Unusually for a concerto, it was sold immediately to the publisher Artaria, who issued it the following August. Many of Mozart's smaller-scale pieces, particularly the dances, were much in demand (ironically enough) by 1791, and 48 dances alone were published that year. It has been estimated that Mozart probably received around 750 gulden from his various publishers in the last year of his life – a sum roughly comparable to Haydn's annual earnings from publications, and by no means meagre. Certainly his financial crisis seems to have been less acute – the begging letters were less frequent – and his spirits had revived. Poverty is only relative, and it must be remembered that Mozart, although frequently 'financially embarrassed', was not actually living in real hardship. But his social position had always required him to keep up appearances, and especially now that he was court kammermusicus he and his wife expected to dress well, entertain their friends, keep a carriage, and domestic help. The popular impression of Mozart literally starving in a cold garret during the last year of his life is, simply, a myth.

In May Mozart petitioned the town council for the (unpaid) post of assistant kapellmeister at St Stephen's Cathedral. By a supreme stroke of irony he got the job, with the possibility of taking over as kapellmeister on the death or retirement of the ageing and sickly incumbent, Leopold Hoffman. However, the old kapellmeister managed to cling on to life for another couple of years, by which time Mozart was himself dead. In celebration of his new appointment Mozart apparently intended to write a large-scale *missa solemnis* in D minor, of which one movement, a Kyrie previously thought to date from much earlier in his career, survives.

In June, Constanze, accompanied by her son Carl and her maid, went as usual to Baden. Mozart had become acquainted with the choirmaster there, Anton Stoll, for whom he wrote the exquisite motet *Ave verum corpus*. Mozart wrote often to his wife, admonishing her not to fall in the baths, not to go out walking alone, and not to gamble in the casino. 'As long as you are well and are nice to me,' he wrote, 'I don't give a damn if everything else goes wrong.' In July Constanze gave birth to their last child, Franz Xaver, who – against all the odds – survived. Wolfgang, meanwhile, was having rather a good time in Vienna on his own, staying sometimes with his friends Leutgeb the horn-player and the Puchbergs, who kept him fed, and going out drinking with an old friend, Emmanuel Schikaneder, an actor, singer, writer and producer and the manager of the Theater auf

ABOVE *The interior of the Theater auf der Wieden, where* The Magic Flute *was premièred in September 1791.*

der Wieden in the suburbs. This was an up-and-coming concern which was beginning to attract Viennese middle class society in large numbers. Schikaneder suggested to Mozart the idea of writing a new kind of opera-pantomime, with German dialogue, for the theatre, in which Schikaneder himself would have a part. It was this opera – *Die Zauberflöte* (The Magic Flute) – which occupied Mozart throughout his last summer in Vienna. 'As soon as my work here is finished', he wrote to Constanze, 'I shall join you, for I intend to take a long rest in your arms; and I shall really need it, for all this mental worry and all the rushing about in connection with it is really wearing me out . . . .' Mozart was by now seriously overworked: he ascribed his periodic fits of depression to his separation from his wife. 'My one wish now is that my business should be finished,' he wrote in a *cri de coeur* on 7 July, 'so that we can be together again. You can't imagine how I have been aching for you . . . I can't describe my feeling – a sort of emptiness, which is dreadfully painful – a sort of longing which cannot be satisfied, but never goes away, indeed it increases daily . . .'

It was while he was in this low state, and working hard to complete *The Magic Flute*, under Schikaneder's constant pressure, that another disquieting commission arrived. He received an unsigned letter, delivered by an unknown messenger, asking him to write a Requiem Mass. Mozart consulted his wife, who advised him to accept. An advance was requested and paid, and a further sum promised on delivery, so long as Mozart made no attempt to discover its source. According to another version of events, Mozart was visited by a 'mysterious stranger' who offered him the commission on behalf of an anonymous patron, producing the initial fee immediately. There was, in fact, no real 'mystery': the commission was from a Viennese nobleman, Count Walsegg-Stuppach, an amateur musician and composer. The count had a penchant for asking various well-known composers to write chamber works for him – for which they were handsomely paid – and then pretending to his friends that he himself was the composer. There was not yet an established concept of intellectual property and to the count there seemed no harm in the deception; it was simply an innocent amusement. On 14 February 1791 he had lost his young wife, Anna, to whom he was devoted. As a memorial to her he decided to commission a Requiem Mass, to be performed on the anniversary of her death; but, as usual, he wanted to keep the real composer's name a secret. Mozart was the unwitting victim of his little scheme.

Shortly after beginning work on the *Requiem*, Mozart received another, equally unexpected commission. Leopold II was to be crowned King of Bohemia in Prague in October, and a suitable opera was hastily required – in less than two months. The Prague impresario Guardasoni was given the unenviable task of getting one together. His first choice for composer had been the imperial court composer Salieri, who for complicated reasons was obliged to decline the offer. So

Guardasoni asked his old friend Mozart, who accepted, for a fee of 250 ducats. There was no time to write a libretto from scratch, so Guardasoni proposed an adaptation of Metastasio's *La clemenza di Tito* (the Clemency of Titus) which was generally felt to be suitable for the occasion. Since the imperial poet Da Ponte had fallen out of favour at the Viennese court, and had left in disgrace, his temporary successor Caterino Mazzolà was asked to freshen up the old warhorse for a new setting, while Guardasoni rushed to Italy to find suitable singers.

Mozart began work on *Tito* in late July, not knowing at that stage who the singers were going to be. He and Constanze left for Prague on 25 August, once more leaving a tiny baby behind, and taking Mozart's pupil Franz Xaver Süssmayr with them to help with the composition. Mozart and he wrote most of the opera in the stage-coach. From beginning to end its composition took 18 days – the kind of speedwriting record only surpassed by Rossini. It was first performed on 6 September.

La Clemenza di Tito is one of the last of the *opere serie*, a genre which by then had fallen more or less totally out of fashion. Even Mozart failed to infuse new life into its moribund form. It remains a superb *pièce d'occasion*, and is only rarely revived today. The plot concerns an attempt to assassinate the Roman Emperor Titus: it is foiled, but the magnanimous emperor pardons the conspirators. The scoring is suitably opulent, with pairs of clarinets or their dark-hued relatives, basset-horns, augmenting the woodwind section; but despite some magnificent individual arias the opera was not a success. One member of the audience described it as 'boring', and the singers were indifferent. After the glittering state occasion of the première, which of course was full, it played to empty houses, while the Prague public continued to flock to *Don Giovanni*, then currently enjoying a revival.

On returning to Vienna at the end of September, Constanze immediately left for Baden, while Mozart put the finishing touches to *The Magic Flute*. On 30 September, the day that *Tito* had its last performance in Prague, the new opera opened at the Theater auf der Wieden.

At face value, *The Magic Flute* is a musical fairy-tale with a rather silly plot, cooked up by Schikaneder from a variety of sources. The story concerns the efforts of Prince Tamino to rescue Pamina, daughter of the Queen of the Night, from the wicked magician Sarastro who has abducted her. But halfway through, in a confusing volte-face, Sarastro turns out to represent the forces of good, and the Queen of the Night those of darkness and evil. Tamino and Pamina are eventually united, having first undergone various trials to test their resolution and moral courage: only then can they join the ranks of the Enlightened Ones. As always, there are sub-plots involving comic characters, of whom the most memorable is the bird-catcher Papageno (played by Schikaneder himself). For him, Mozart wrote some of his most overtly tuneful and appealing songs such as 'Der Vögelfänger bin

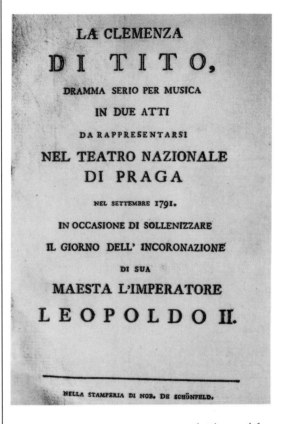

ABOVE *The title page of the libretto of* La clemenza di Tito.

ich ja', 'Ein Mädchen oder Weibchen', and the delightful duet with Pamina, 'Bei Männern welche Liebe fühlen'. Coloratura brilliance is represented in this opera by the Queen of the Night's two arias, of which 'Der hölle Rache' is a showpiece of virtuosity whose stratospheric high notes have proved the downfall of many an aspiring soprano. (She was played first by Mozart's sister-in-law, Josepha.) The music for the two lovers is predominantly lyrical, rather than heroic, as befits a Singspiel. Pamina's G minor aria 'Ach, ich fühls', in which she laments the apparent loss of Tamino's love, is one of the simplest, yet most heartfelt musical expressions of grief ever penned.

So far, *The Magic Flute* appears to fit neatly into the Viennese Singspiel tradition, with its emphasis on simple music, and dramatic effects (monsters, choruses of dancing slaves, etc.) drawn from pantomime. But scratch the surface, and an astonishing mystery is revealed. When the first-night audience studied their printed librettos, they may have been intrigued by the curious frontispiece. The scene depicted seems vaguely Egyptian in style, but closer examination reveals that it is spattered with Masonic symbols – a pyramid covered with hieroglyphics, a chain with a five-pointed star, a trowel, a pair of compasses, and an hour-glass. (This frontispiece was later suppressed.) And, having digested that, any Masons would have shot out of their seats at the beginning of the overture – threefold chords in a knocking rhythm. (The three knocks were a central feature of the Masonic ritual, though Mozart's dotted rhythm was specific to a Parisian lodge, the Grand Orient.)

But that was not all. The opera is permeated with the Masonic sacred number – three. It is in the key of E flat major, which has three flats; there are three Ladies, attendants to the Queen of the Night, and three Spirits, who are sent to guide Tamino to Pamina. The rituals Tamino and Papageno are required to undergo, which include taking vows of fasting and silence, have exact parallels in the initiation ceremonies which an apprentice Mason undergoes on the way to becoming a Master. The famous scene of the Men in Armour, leading to the final ordeals of fire and water, are drawn from even higher Masonic rituals, while the closing chorus actually contains the three words 'Weisheit, Schönheit, Stärke' (wisdom, beauty, strength) which would have appeared in the end-of-meeting rituals used by Mozart's own lodge. Symbolism even more arcane, such as the emphasis on the number 18 (possibly a reference to the 18th French Rose-Croix Degree) has been noted in the opera by the Mozart scholar H. C. Robbins Landon, quite apart from the obvious overall Enlightenment theme of the passage from the darkness of ignorance to the light of knowledge, and the apparent identification of Sarastro, priest of wisdom, with the eminent scientist Ignaz von Born, Master of the Viennese lodge Zur wahren Eintracht. Even Masonic anti-feminism surfaces in *The Magic Flute*: the Queen of the Night is condemned for

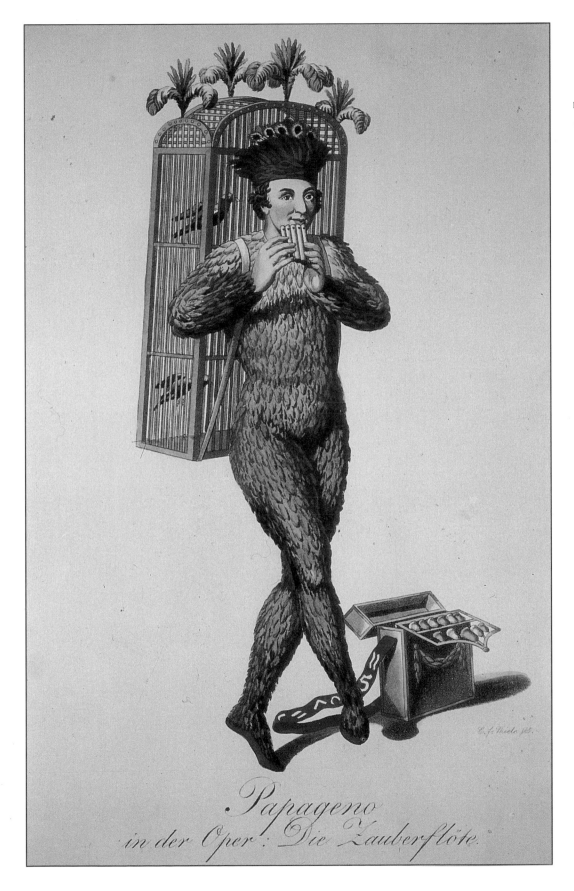

Papageno
in der Oper: Die Zauberflöte.

LEFT *Papageno – the role was first played by Schikaneder – from* The Magic Flute.

ABOVE *The initiation scene from Act II of* The Magic Flute.

ABOVE *The opening scene of*
The Magic Flute.

over-ambition; while her daughter's trials are far greater than Tamino's – at least he understands why he is obliged to undergo them, while Pamina is told nothing and is expected to bear her tribulations patiently and obediently until redeemed by the love of a good man. She is a far cry indeed from the wily, self-sufficient Susanna of *Figaro*!

All this overt symbolism leads to one inescapable conclusion: Mozart and Schikaneder had decided to write a 'Masonic' opera. Since, as we have seen, both were bound on pain of dreadful punishments not to reveal the secrets of their Order, why did they do it? It has been suggested that the Masons took a terrible revenge for the

BELOW *Sarastro's entrance from* The Magic Flute.

revelations of *The Magic Flute* and brought about Mozart's death; but Schikaneder, who was equally guilty, escaped unscathed. The latest theory, persuasively put forward by Professor Landon, is that the opera represented a last-ditch attempt to *preserve* the rituals of the Order against the anti-Masonic machinations of the emperor and his secret police, and to present the movement to the general public for what it was – a noble institution under threat from the forces of reaction. But if that was the intention, it failed. Within three years, the Masonic movement in Austria had been eliminated.

After initially arousing astonishment, *The Magic Flute* caught the public's imagination. Mozart wrote to Constanze that it was attracting full houses, and several numbers – 'Mann und Weib', Papageno's glockenspiel in the Act One finale, and the trio of the three boys from Act II ('Sied uns zum zweiten Mal willkommen') had to be repeated. But what Mozart enjoyed most was the 'silent approval' – could he mean that of the Masons? In another letter he describes how he impishly tried to put Schikaneder's nose out of joint by playing the glockenspiel out of time from the wings. Only then, said Mozart, did many of the audience realize that Papageno was not actually playing the instrument himself.

The very last letter Mozart wrote, dated 14 October 1791, is particularly touching. We know quite a lot about him as a son and a husband, but little about his feelings as a parent – he makes no reference in his surviving letters to the deaths of four of his children. Little Carl Mozart, then seven-years-old, had been sent to school in Perchtholdsdorf, a suburb of Vienna, and Mozart drove out on 13 October to collect him and take him and his grandmother Weber to see a performance of *The Magic Flute*. Mozart reported to Constanze that Carl loved the opera (which was also attended that night by his old enemy Salieri), and then went on to discuss the shortcomings of Carl's education – just like any other anxious parent. 'If anything, he is even less inclined to learn than before . . . he just runs wild in the garden for ten hours a day.'

While Mozart's offspring, both physical and spiritual, flourished, he himself slid into a decline. By now chronically ill, and exhausted by his summer's overwork, he had no resistance left to the sudden change in climate which hit Vienna in the late autumn, with freezing fog, snow and biting winds. On returning from Prague, Mozart had completed his last instrumental piece, the exquisitely melancholy Clarinet Concerto (originally written for basset-horn), for his friend Anton Stadler, and in early November he wrote a short cantata, *Kleine Freimaurer-Kantate*, K.623, for a Masonic meeting. But his main preoccupation was with the unfinished *Requiem*, which had begun to prey on his mind. According to a posthumous account of Mozart's last months, he and Constanze drove out to the Prater one fine day at the end of October, during which Mozart told his wife that he was convinced he was writing his own Requiem. It seems to have been about then that he mentioned for the first time that he thought he was being poisoned with *acqua toffana* (a notorious Italian poison). Constanze, thoroughly alarmed, forbade him to do any more work on the *Requiem* until his health improved. But on 20 November, his condition worsened, and he took to his bed. With Süssmayr's help, he did what work he could on the *Requiem*, completing the Introitus in full score, and sketching the bulk of the rest, to the end of the Hostias, in short score (giving only details of instrumentation). The work was not

ABOVE *The original, suppressed frontispiece to the libretto of* The Magic Flute, *showing the Masonic symbols.*

107

written in liturgical order, and Mozart's own part in it breaks off after eight bars of the Lachrymosa. The work was 'completed' after Mozart's death by Süssmayr along with another of his young protégés, Joseph Eybler, and a local composer, F. J. Freystädtler.

Mozart's final illness lasted 15 days, during which time his body swelled, he vomited intermittently and he suffered from high fever. Three days before he died, in a master-stroke of irony, the emperor confirmed his appointment as kapellmeister at St Stephen's – a post which would have brought him a steady income of 2,000 gulden a year. According to Constanze, he received the news with painful resignation, saying that the situation would have enabled him for the first time to have sufficient leisure to write what he wanted, and to justify his growing reputation; but instead only death awaited him.

The heart-rending description of Mozart's death was left by Sophie, Constanze's younger sister. On Saturday, 3 December, Mozart seemed better and more cheerful. On the 4th, Sophie, who normally visited her sister every day to help out, decided not to go, but to go out for a walk instead. She went to the kitchen to make coffee, but at that moment her lamp suddenly went out, and she was seized with a dreadful feeling of foreboding. She hurried round to Mozart's apartment, where she found Constanze in a terrible state, though trying to keep calm. Wolfgang's condition had worsened, and he told Sophie that he had the 'taste of death' on his tongue. Constanze sent Sophie to fetch her mother and a priest – who took hours to come. On returning to the apartment, Sophie found Mozart in a high fever, trying to explain to Süssmayr how to complete the *Requiem*. Sophie went to fetch the family doctor, who was at the theatre. He applied cold poultices to the sufferer's forehead, which sent him into a coma. Just before one o'clock on Monday morning, 5 December 1791, the greatest composer the world has ever known finally found the 'long rest' he needed so desperately.

X
Aftermath: The Legend

T HE IMMEDIATE AFTERMATH of music history's greatest tragedy was despair and confusion. The grief-stricken widow refused to leave her dead husband's side, and even crawled into his bed in a vain attempt to infect herself with his disease. Someone from the Vienna art gallery arrived to take a death mask, and crowds of people were soon queuing to view the body, which was laid on a bier in a black suit with a cowl over its head. Later, friends persuaded Constanze to leave the apartment and take temporary refuge with one of Mozart's fellow-Masons.

The cause of Mozart's death was registered as 'acute miliary fever'. His son Carl later recalled that a few days before his father's death there was already a terrible stench of decomposition, the advanced state of which apparently made an autopsy impossible. Since Constanze had very little money, it was recommended that Mozart's corpse be given the cheapest available funeral. On 6 December, as soon as was decently possible, it was conveyed in a funeral wagon to St Stephen's Cathedral, where it was met by the funeral party and blessed by the priest in a chapel on the north side. The benediction was given in the cathedral itself, before Mozart began his last journey, alone, to the burial ground of St Marx. The weather was not wild and stormy, as has sometimes been suggested, but mild for the time of year. However none of the mourners (who apparently included Salieri) wanted to undertake the hour's walk to the cemetery. Mozart was buried in the customary way in an unmarked mass grave, and its exact location has never been discovered.

One of Mozart's contemporaries summed up what were probably the feelings of many fellow-musicians on hearing the news of his death: it was, of course, a pity that such a great genius was dead, but on the whole it was a good thing for the others. 'If he had lived any longer, the world wouldn't have given a toss for any of our compositions.'

Well over 30 years later, renewed speculation as to the cause of Mozart's premature death was prompted by an extraordinary confession said to have been made by Salieri – then in his 70s, extremely ill, and

LEFT A *bronze figurine depicting the young Mozart.*

mentally unstable. Salieri had never got on with Leopold II, and in 1790 he had been released from most of his court obligations, remaining as a kind of honorary kapellmeister. His confession – that he had been responsible for poisoning Mozart – has intrigued historians and musicians ever since, but it seems to be quite unfounded. The latest medical theories suggest that Mozart's last illness had its roots in the various serious infections he had suffered as a child: on the early trip to Paris and London he had contracted rheumatic fever, tonsillitis, and typhoid fever; in 1767 he had caught smallpox; and in Italy he seems to have had bronchitis and yellow jaundice. He continued to suffer from periodic chest infections throughout his early manhood; but the earliest symptoms of his terminal illness appeared in 1784, when he was attacked by violent colic, vomiting, and rheumatic fever, resulting from a virus caught during an epidemic. This may have left him with a condition known as Schönlein-Henoch Syndrome, together with the beginnings of chronic kidney disease. For the last four years of his life he suffered periodic attacks of the same symptoms, which damaged his kidneys still further, and led to high blood pressure. He actually died of kidney failure, set off by a viral infection probably contracted during a Masonic meeting in mid-November. He was subjected to the common medical practice of bleeding, which weakened him further, and a massive cerebral haemorrhage finally killed him.

Salieri's 'admission' may thus be discounted as the ravings of a demented old man. Nonetheless, he may well have had a guilty conscience: he certainly tried to use his influence to poison Mozart's career, out of sheer jealousy at the younger man's superior talents; but he does not seem to have been directly involved in his death. Besides, it is highly unlikely that a murderer would attend his victim's funeral.

The day after Mozart's death, his friend and fellow-Mason Franz Hofdemel attacked his pregnant wife, Magdalene, with a razor, severely injuring her, and then killed himself. Rumours abounded that the reason was that Magdalene (a pupil of Mozart's) had also been the composer's mistress, and that her unborn child was Mozart's. Likewise, various scurrilous attacks were made on Constanze's honour, suggesting that during her frequent sojourns in Baden she had taken Mozart's pupil Süssmayr as a lover, and that her last child (who bore Süssmayr's Christian names) was his. There seems to be absolutely no foundation to either tale.

After her initial prostration, Constanze proved remarkably resilient, and began to demonstrate her innate capacity for organization. Within a week she had applied to the court for a widow's pension. Although by rights she was not eligible, Mozart not having fulfilled his qualifying period of 10 years' court service, the emperor was inclined to be generous. Constanze eventually received one third of her husband's former salary. Meanwhile she had many friends who took up her cause: memorial concerts were given in Prague and Vienna; she received a gratuity from the Elector of Cologne; and the King of Prussia offered to purchase several compositions for 100 ducats each (including the *Requiem* which Constanze made sure was 'completed' by Süssmayr so that she could collect the last instalment of money due from Count Walsegg). The original score – the two movements completed by Mozart, and the rest added by Süssmayr in a hand almost indistinguishable (deliberately so) from Mozart's – was given to Count Walsegg, who for once found himself on the receiving end of a little deception. About 10 years after his death, in 1838, the score was discovered in the castle archives, and sold to the imperial court library. The *Requiem* was first publicly performed on 2 January 1793, and the receipts donated to Constanze.

She, meanwhile, devoted herself to selling as many of her husband's

BELOW *Mozart's memorial statue in Salzburg.*

works as she could to various publishers, including J. A. André of Offenbach am Main, and Breitkopf & Härtel of Leipzig. In 1794 and 1795 she organized concert performances of *La clemenza di Tito* in Vienna (in the 1795 performance Beethoven played the D minor Piano Concerto, K.466, between the acts); and then took it on tour through Germany, with great success. She also tried hard to revive interest in *Idomeneo*, thus proving that she was no musical ignoramus.

In 1797 Constanze, then 36 years old, met a Danish diplomat, Georg Nikolaus Nissen. They became friends, then lovers, and finally, in 1809, husband and wife. Nissen took a personal interest in Constanze's crusade on behalf of Mozart's music, and helped her a great deal. 20 years later the English publisher Vincent Novello and his wife Mary visited Salzburg where Constanze (once again widowed) and Mozart's sister were both living. They found Nannerl (then in her late 70s) 'blind, languid, feeble, exhausted and nearly speechless', but were most impressed with Constanze, whom they thought 'a well-bred lady' and 'a delightful woman'. Constanze was only too happy to recall the days of her first marriage, and she pointed out Mozart's own favourite numbers from the operas, including Cherubino's 'Non so più' and the sextet 'Riconosci a questo amplesso' from *Figaro*; 'Di scrivermi', the second quintet from *Così fan tutte*; and the Commendatore's music from *Don Giovanni*.

All contemporary accounts of Constanze's character, except those originating from Leopold and Nannerl Mozart (neither of whom ever really accepted her), together with the evidence of Mozart's own letters to her, confirm that she made him as good a wife as he could have wished. It cannot be easy to be the partner of a genius, and Constanze certainly made the best of it. She lived to be 80.

Of her two surviving children, Carl showed no particular musical aptitude. He became a civil servant in Milan, and died in 1858, aged 74. Franz Xaver, only six months old when his father died, was later sent to study music in Prague, where he lived with the Dušeks. Constanze attempted to launch him on a career similar to his father's – as a child-prodigy pianist – and on returning to Vienna he took composition lessons with Salieri, who proclaimed his 'a rare talent'. Not rare enough, unfortunately. Franz Xaver later toured Europe as a concert pianist, and published a large amount of piano and vocal music, all of which has sunk without trace. He died in Carlsbad shortly after his 53rd birthday. There are now no living descendants of the Mozart family.

The house in which Mozart died in Vienna – No 970 Rauhenstein-gasse – no longer exists: it was demolished in the 19th century and is now the site of the Steffel department store. The list of Mozart's effects, made immediately after his death, included books, manu-scripts, a billiard table, a fortepiano, a 'viola in its own case' (his violin must have remained at Salzburg), as well as the usual pieces of

IOHANN ANDRÉ.

TOP *J A André (1741–99) founded his own publishing firm in Offenbach am Main. He published many of Mozart's works after the composer's death.*

ABOVE *Mozart's violin.*

furniture and various personal effects. Some of these, including the fortepiano, are now in the Mozart museum (the Mozarteum) at Salzburg, located in the house where he was born.

Mozart was by no means forgotten after his death: on the contrary, his reputation continued to spread widely as his music became available through publications and performances of the operas (especially *The Magic Flute* and *Don Giovanni*). In 1798 Breitkopf & Härtel launched the first 'collected edition' of Mozart's works, and the first biography (Niemetschek's *Life of Kapellmeister Wolfgang Gottlieb Mozart written from Original Sources*) appeared in Prague. 30 years later, Constanze's husband Georg Nissen published another biography, based on his wife's recollections; but the first scholarly biography did not appear until the centenary of his birth. Six years later, in 1862, Köchel published the first edition of his famous thematic catalogue, which itself stimulated a 'complete edition' of the music, published between 1877 and 1883 by Breitkopf. The bicentenary of Mozart's birth gave rise to the instigation of a new complete edition – the 'Neue Mozart Ausgabe' – which continues today.

The 20th century has seen Mozart's reputation rise ever higher, with new scholarly publications appearing every year, and public appetite for information on the man and his music increasing all the time. The great Da Ponte operas have been constantly in the international repertory since the early years of the century (with the exception of *Così fan tutte*, which finally came back into its own in the 1950s); while the lesser-known ones such as *Idomeneo* and *La clemenza di Tito* are now taking their place alongside their more familiar stablemates. Scholars continue to unearth new facts and new material: one of the most exciting events of the 1980s was the almost accidental rediscovery in Kraków, Poland, of a substantial number of major autograph manuscripts (including *The Magic Flute*, the C minor Mass, and the 'Jupiter' Symphony) which had disappeared from the Prussian State Library in Berlin during the Second World War, and which were feared lost for ever.

Also in the 1980s, Peter Schaffer's brilliant and thought-provoking play (and film) *Amadeus* has made Mozart's a household name, and his music familiar to millions. Though it mixes fact with fantasy, the play contains some fascinating meditations on the nature of genius, and has awakened an extraordinary surge of interest in the life and work of the man who still, 200 years after his death, stands supreme on a pinnacle of his art. For this 'miracle that God let be born in Salzburg', every musician has since humbly given thanks.

SELECTIVE WORKLIST

Unless otherwise stated, only complete, authentic works are included. K numbers refer to Köchel's thematic catalogue (see Bibliography).

A. Vocal

1. Dramatic works

Apollo et Hyacinthus *Latin intermezzo*	K.38	1767	
La finta semplice *opera buffa*	K.51	1768–9	
Bastien und Bastienne *Singspiel*	K.50	1768	
Mitridate, rè di Ponto *opera seria*	K.87	1770	
Ascanio in Alba *festa teatrale*	K.111	1771	
Il sogno di Scipione *serenata*	K.126	1772	
Lucio Silla *opera seria*	K.135	1772	
La finta giardiniera *opera buffa*	K.196	1775	
Il rè pastore *dramma per musica*	K.208	1775	
Thamos, König in Ägypten *incidental music*	K.345	1776–9	
Zaïde *Singspiel*	K.344	1779–80	*(incomplete)*
Idomeneo, rè di Creta *opera seria*	K.366	1781	
Die Entführung aus dem Serail *Singspiel*	K.384	1782	
L'oca del Cairo *opera buffa*	K.422	?1783	*(incomplete)*
Lo sposo deluso *opera buffa*	K.430	?1783	*(incomplete)*
Der Schauspieldirektor *Singspiel*	K.486	1786	
Le nozze di Figaro *opera buffa*	K.492	1786	
Don Giovanni *opera buffa*	K.527	1787	
Così fan tutte *opera buffa*	K.588	1790	
Die Zauberflöte *Singspiel*	K.620	1791	
La clemenza di Tito *opera seria*	K.621	1791	

2. Oratorios, cantatas, etc.

Die Schuldigkeit des ersten Gebots *oratorio*	K.35	1767
Grabmusik *cantata*	K.42	1767
La Betulia liberata *oratorio*	K.118	1771
Davidde penitente *oratorio*	K.469	1785
Die Maurerfreude *Masonic cantata*	K.471	1785
Die ihr des unermesslichen Weltalls Schöpfer ehrt *Masonic cantata*	K.619	1791
Eine kleine Freimaurer-Kantate *Masonic cantata*	K.623	1791

3. *Sacred music*

Masses

9 Missae breves: in G, K.19, 1768; in D minor, K.65, 1769; in G, K.140, 1773; in F, K.192 1774; in D, K.194, 1774; in C, K.220, 1775–6; in C, K.258, 1776; in C, K.259, 1776 ('Organ Solo Mass'); in B flat, K.275, 1777

Missa solemnis in C minor ('Waisenhausmesse') K.139, 1768

Mass in C ('Dominicus'), K.66, 1769

Mass in C ('In honorem Ssmae Trinitatis'), K.167, 1773

Mass in C, K.262, 1775

Mass in C ('Credo'), K.257, 1776

Mass in C ('Coronation'), K.317, 1779

Missa solemnis in C, K.337, 1780

Mass in C minor, K.427, 1782–3 *(incomplete)*

Requiem in D minor, K.626, 1791 *(unfinished)*

2 Kyries, in F, K.33, 1766; in D minor, K.341, 1788 or 1791

4. *Other sacred vocal*

2 Litaniae Lauretanae BVM: in B flat, K.109, 1771; in D, K.195, 1774

2 Litaniae de venerabili altaris sacramento: in B flat, K.125, 1772; in E flat, K.243, 1776

2 Vespers: Vesperae de Dominica in C, K.321, 1779

Vesperae solennes de confessore in C, K.339, 1780

Dixit Dominus and Magnificat in C, K.193, 1774

c20 motets and antiphons, including

God is our refuge in G minor, K.20, 1765; Te Deum in C, K.141, 1769; 3 Regina coeli: in C, K.108, 1771; in B flat, K.127, 1772; in C, K.276, 1779; Exsultate, jubilate, K.165, 1773; Ave verum corpus, K.618, 1791

5. *Secular vocal*

c55 concert arias with orchestra

6 vocal ensembles with orchestra

9 vocal ensembles with piano or instrumental accompaniment

c30 solo songs with keyboard, including Der Zauberer, K.472, 1785; Die Zufriedenheit, K.473, 1785; Die betrogene Welt, K.474, 1785; Das Veilchen, K.476, 1785; Lied der Freiheit, K.506, 1785; Die Alte, K.517, 1787; Abendempfindung, K.523, 1787; An Chloe, K.524, 1787; Das Traumbild, K.530, 1787; Die kleine Spinnerin, K.531, 1787; Sehnsucht nach dem Frühlinge, K.596, 1791; Im Frühlingsanfang, K.597, 1791; Das Kinderspiel, K.598, 1791

Also numerous canons, mostly composed between 1782 and 1788

B.
Orchestral

		1.	*Symphonies*		
in E flat	NO 1	K.16	1764–5	
in A minor		K.16A	1760s	
in D	NO 4	K.19	1765	
in F		K.19A	1765	
in B flat	NO 5	K.22	1765	
in F	NO 6	K.43	1767	
in D	NO 7	K.45	1768	
in G		K.45A	c1765	'Lambach'
in B flat		K.45B	1768	
in D	NO 8	K.48	1768	
in C	NO 9	K.73	1772	
in D		K.81	1770	
in D		K.97	1770	
in D		K.95	1770	
in D	NO 11	K.84	1770	
in G	NO 10	K.74	1770	
in F		K.75	1771	
in G	NO 12	K.110	1771	
in C		K.96	1771	
in F	NO 13	K.112	1771	
in A	NO 14	K.114	1771	
in G	NO 15	K.124	1772	
in C	NO 16	K.128	1772	
in G	NO 17	K.129	1772	
in F	NO 18	K.130	1772	
in E flat	NO 19	K.132	1772	
in D	NO 20	K.133	1772	
in A	NO 21	K.134	1772	
in E flat	NO 26	K.184	1773	
in G	NO 27	K.199	1773	
in C	NO 22	K.162	1773	
in D	NO 23	K.181	1773	
in B flat	NO 24	K.182	1773	
in G minor	NO 25	K.183	1773	
in A	NO 29	K.201	1774	
in D	NO 30	K.202	1774	
in C	NO 28	K.200	1774	
in D	NO 31	K.297	1778	'Paris'
in G	NO 32	K.318	1779	Overture to Zaïde
in B flat	NO 33	K.319	1779	
in C	NO 34	K.338	1780	
in D	NO 35	K.385	1782	'Haffner'
in C	NO 36	K.425	1783	'Linz'
in G	NO 37	K.444	1783–4	introduction to symphony by Michael Haydn
in D	NO 38	K.504	1786	'Prague'
in E flat	NO 39	K.543	1788	
in G minor	NO 40	K.550	1788	
in C	NO 41	K.551	1788	'Jupiter'

2. Serenades, cassations and divertimenti for mixed ensemble

Gallimathius musicum	K.32	1766	
Cassation in D	K.100	1769	
Cassation in G	K.63	1769	
Cassation in B flat	K.99	1769	
Divertimento in E flat	K.113	1771	
Divertimento in D	K.131	1772	
Divertimento in D	K.205	c.1773	
Serenade in D	K.185	1773	
Serenade in D	K.203	1774	
Serenade in D	K.204	1775	
Serenata notturna in D	K.239	1776	
Divertimento in F	K.247	1776	
Serenade in D	K.250	1776	'Haffner'
Divertimento in D	K.251	1776	
Notturno in D	K.286	1776–7	
Divertimento in B flat	K.287	1777	
Serenade in D	K.320	1779	'Posthorn'
Divertimento in D	K.334	1779–80	
Mauererische Trauermusik in C minor	K.477	1785	
Ein musikalischer Spass in F	K.522	1787	
Eine kleine Nachtmusik in G	K.525	1787	

3. Serenades and divertimenti for wind ensemble

Divertimento in B flat	K.186	1773
Divertimento in E flat	K.166	1773
Divertimento in F	K.213	1775
Divertimento in B flat	K.240	1776
Divertimento in E flat	K.252	1776
Divertimento in C	K.188	1773
Divertimento in F	K.253	1776
Divertimento in B flat	K.270	1777
Divertimento in E flat	K.289	1777
Serenade in B flat	K.361	c1781
Serenade in E flat	K.375	1781
Serenade in C minor	K.388	1782–3

5 divertimentos (K.A229), 2 adagios (K.410–11) and 12 duos (K.487) for mixed clarinets and basset-horns

4. Concertos

23 original piano concertos (excluding arrangements)

in D	NO 5	K.175	1773	
in B flat	NO 6	K.238	1776	
in F	NO 7	K.242	1776	(for 3 pianos)
in C	NO 8	K.246	1776	
in E flat	NO 9	K.271	1777	
in E flat	NO 10	K.365	1779	(for 2 pianos)
in F	NO 11	K.413	c1782–3	
in A	NO 12	K.414	1782	
in C	NO 13	K.415	1782–3	
in E flat	NO 14	K.449	1784	
in B flat	NO 15	K.450	1784	
in D	NO 16	K.451	1784	
in G	NO 17	K.453	1784	
in B flat	NO 18	K.456	1784	
in F	NO 19	K.459	1784	
in D minor	NO 20	K.466	1785	
in C	NO 21	K.467	1785	
in E flat	NO 22	K.482	1785	
in A	NO 23	K.488	1786	
in C minor	NO 24	K.491	1786	
in C	NO 25	K.503	1786	
in D	NO 26	K.537	1788	'Coronation'
in B flat	NO 27	K.595	1788–91	

2 concert rondos for piano and orchestra: in D, K.382, 1782 (new finale for Concerto in D, K.175); in A, K.386, 1782

Concertos for strings

Concertone for 2 violins	in C	K.190	1774
5 violin concertos	in B flat	K.207	1773
	in D	K.211	1775
	in G	K.216	1775
	in D	K.218	1775
	in A	K.219	1775
Sinfonia Concertante for violin and viola	in E flat	K.364	1779
2 rondos for violin and orchestra	in B flat	K.269	1776
	in C	K.373	1781
Adagio for violin and orchestra	in E	K.261	1776

Concertos for wind

Concerto for bassoon	in B flat	K.191	1774
Concerto for flute	in G	K.313	1778
Concerto for flute or oboe	in C or D	K.314	1778
Concerto for flute and harp	in C	K.299	1778
4 horn concertos	in D	K.412	1791
	in E flat	K.417	1783
	in E flat	K.447	1784–7
	in E flat	K.495	1786
Concerto for clarinet	in A	K.622	1791
Andante for flute	in C	K.315	1779–80

---

5. Dance music

13 marches for orchestra, 1769–82

c103 minuets for orchestra, including
set of 7, K.65A, 1769; set of 19, K.103, 1772; set of 6, K.104, 1770–1; set of 6, K.164, 1772; set of 16, K.176, 1773; set of 3, K.363, 1782–3; set of 6, K.461, 1784; set of 12, K.568, 1788; set of 12, K.585, 1789; set of 6, K.599, 1791; set of 4, K.601, 1791; set of 2, K.604, 1791

56 German dances, including
set of 6, K.509, 1787; set of 6, K.536, 1788; set of 6, K.567, 1788; set of 6, K.571, 1789; set of 12, K.586, 1789; set of 6, K.600, 1791; set of 4, K.602, 1791; set of 3, K.605, 1791; set of 6, K.606, 1791; Die Leyerer in C, K.605, 1791

36 contredanses, including
set of 4, K.101, 1776; set of 4, K.267, 1777; set of 6, K.462, 1784; set of 2, K.463, 1784; Das Donnerwetter, K.534, 1788; La bataille, K.535, 1788; Der Sieg vom Helden Coburg, K.587, 1789; set of 3, K.106, 1790; set of 2, K.603, 1791; Il trionfo delle dame, K.607, 1791; set of 5, K.609, 1791; Les filles malicieuses, K.610, 1791

---

6. Ballet music

Les petits riens K.A10, 1778

---

7. Works for organ and orchestra

3 church sonatas in C for organ and orchestra: K.263, 1776; K.278, 1777; K.329, 1779
14 church sonatas for organ and strings, 1772–80

C. Chamber Music

1.	Strings and wind

4 quartets for flute, violin, viola and cello

in D	K.285	1777
in G	K.285A	1778
in C	K.A171	?1781–2
in A	K.298	1786–7

Quartet for oboe, violin, viola and cello in F, K.370, 1781

Quintet for horn, violin, 2 violas and cello in E flat, K.407, 1782

Quintet for clarinet, 2 violins, viola and cello in A, K.581, 1789

Duo for bassoon and cello in B flat, K.292, 1775

2. Strings

6 string quintets (2 violins, 2 violas, cello)

in B flat	K.174	1773
in C	K.515	1787
in G minor	K.516	1787
in C minor	K.406	1788
in D	K.593	1790
in E flat	K.614	1791

26 string quartets

	in G	K.80	1770
3 Divertimentos in D, B flat, F,		K.136–8,	1772
	in D	K.155	1772
	in G	K.156	1772
	in C	K.157	1772–3
	in F	K.158	1772–3
	in B flat	K.159	1773
	in E flat	K.160	1773
	in F	K.168	1773
	in A	K.169	1773
	in C	K.170	1773
	in E flat	K.171	1773
	in B flat	K.172	1773
	in D minor	K.173	1773

6 'Haydn' Quartets published (Vienna, 1785) as Op. 10:
in G, K.387, 1782; in D minor, K.421, 1783; in E flat, K.428, 1783; in B flat, K.458 ('Hunt'), 1784; in A, K.464, 1785, in C, K.465 ('Dissonance'), 1785

Quartet in D, K.499 ('Hoffmeister'), 1786

3 'Prussian' Quartets
in D, K.575, 1789; in B flat, K.589, 1790; in F, K.590, 1790

String ensemble

2 sonatas for violin and bass: in C, K.46D; in F, K.46E, 1768
Trio for 2 violins and bass in B flat, K.266, 1777
2 duos for violin and viola: in G, K.423; in B flat, K.424, 1783
Trio for violin, viola and cello in E flat, K.563, 1788

3. Keyboard and ensemble

7 trios for piano, violin and cello: in B flat ('Divertimento'), K.254, 1776; in D minor, K.442, ?1783–90; in G, K.496, 1786; in B flat, K.502, 1786; in E, K.542, 1788; in C, K.548, 1788; in G, K.564, 1788

2 quartets for piano, violin, viola and cello: in G minor, K.478, 1785; in E flat, K. 493, 1786

Quintet for piano, oboe, clarinet, bassoon and horn in E flat, K.452, 1784
Trio for piano, clarinet and viola in E flat, K.498, 1786, 'Kegelstatt'

4. Keyboard and violin

36 sonatas for keyboard and violin, including

2 published as Op.1 (Paris, 1764); in C, K.6, in D, K.7
2 published as Op.2 (Paris, 1764); in B flat, K.8, in G, K.9
6 published as Op.3 (London, 1765); in B flat, G, A, F, C, B flat, K.10–15, (also as flute sonatas)
6 published as Op.4 (The Hague, 1766); in E flat, G, C, D, F, B flat, K.26–31
6 published as 'Op.1' (Paris, 1778); in G, E flat, C, E minor, A, D K.301–6
6 published as 'Op.2' (Vienna, 1781): in F, K.376; in C, K.296; in F, K.377; in B flat, K.378; in G, K.379; in E flat, K.380

Sonata in B flat, K.454, 1784, published (Vienna, 1784), as Op. 7 No 3
Sonata in E flat, K.481, 1785, published (Vienna, 1786)
Sonata in A, K.526, 1787, published (Vienna, 1787)
Sonata in F, K.547, 1788, 'Für Anfänger'

5. Miscellaneous chamber

For mechanical organ
Adagio and Allegro in F minor, K.594, 1790
Fantasia in F minor, K.608, 1791
Andante in F, K.616, 1791

Adagio and Rondo in C minor for glass harmonica, flute, oboe, viola and cello, K.617, 1791
Adagio in C for glass harmonica, K.356, 1791

1. Sonatas

18 solo piano sonatas
No 1 in C, K.279, 1775; No 2 in F, K.280, 1775; No 3 in B flat, K.281, 1775; No 4 in E flat, K.282, 1775; No 5 in G, K.283, 1775; No 6 in D, K.284, 1775; No 7 in C, K.309, 1777; No 8 in A minor, K.310, 1778; No 9 in D, K.311, 1777; No 10 in C, K.330, 1781–3; No 11 in A, K.331, 1781–3; No 12 in F, K.332, 1781–3; No 13 in B flat, K.333, 1783–4; No 14 in C minor, K.457, 1784, published with Fantasia, K.475 (Vienna, 1785); No 15 in F, K.533, 1788; No 16 in C, K.545, 1788 ('Für Anfänger'); No 17 in B flat, K.570, 1789 ; No 18 in D, K.576, 1789

5 sonatas for piano duet
in C, K.19D, 1765; in D, K.381, 1772; in B flat, K.358, 1773–4; in F, K.497, 1786; in C, K.521, 1787

Sonata for 2 pianos in D, K.448, 1781

2. Variations

16 sets of variations for solo keyboard, including

Ah, vous dirai-je, maman in C, K.265, 1781–2; *La belle françoise*, in E flat, K.353, 1781–2; *Lison dormait*, in C, K.264, 1778; *Unser dummer Pöbel meint*, in G, K.455, 1784

1 set of variations for piano duet on an original theme, in G, K.501, 1786

3. Miscellaneous keyboard

40 pieces for solo keyboard, including
8 minuets, K.315A, 1773; Fantasia in C minor, K.475, published with Sonata in C minor, K.457; Rondo in D, K.485, 1786; Rondo in F, K.494, 1786; Rondo in A minor, K.511, 1787; Adagio in B minor, K.540, 1788

Index

Figures in *italics* refer to relevant captions.

Credits

Select Bibliography

Key: *l* = left; *r* = right; *t* = top; *b* = bottom.

The author and publishers have made every effort to identify the copyright owners of the pictures used in this publication; they apologize for any omissions and would like to thank the following:

Courtesy Austrian Tourist Office, London: pages 14*r*, 15, 39, 112. **The Bridgeman Art Library:** pages 18*b*, (Christies, London), 19 (Guildhall Library, London), 21*b* (Oscar & Peter Johnson Ltd, London), 28/29 National Gallery, London), 33*b* (Christies, London), 34/35 (Gavin Graham Gallery, London), 45 (Musée de Versailles, France), 47 (Musée Carnavalet, Paris), 48/49 (Christies, London), 51*b* (Musée Carnavalet, Paris), 62 (Guildhall Art Gallery, London), 94/95 (Victoria & Albert Museum, London), 96 (Schwerin Museum, Germany). **Reproduced by courtesy of the Trustees of the British Museum:** pages 7, 58*t*, endpapers. **Alfred Cortot Collection, Lausanne:** page 27*b*. **E T Archive:** pages 8 (Vienna Societa Amici della Musica), 11 (Vienna Societa Amici della Musica), 18*t*, 20, 21*t* (London Museum), 22, 25 (Vienna Societa Amici della Musica), 30/31 (Biblioteca Esiense, Modena), 42/43, 44 (Musée Carnavalet), 71 (Museum der Stadt Wien), 73, 75 (French Embassy, London), 77*b* (Museum der Stadt, Wien), 78 (Vienna Societa Amici della Musica), 84 (Museum Theatre, London), 87 (Vienna Societa Amici della Musica). **Mary Evans Picture Library:** pages 14*l*, 58*b*, 59, 90, 103, 104, 105. **Geselschaft der Musikfreunde, Vienna:** page 12. **Giraudon/Bridgeman:** pages 23 (Château de Versailles, France), 50 (Château de Versailles, France). **Graphische Sammlung, Munich:** pages 52*t*, 67. **Historisches Museum der Stadt Wien:** page 16. **Internationale Stiftung Mozarteum, Salzburg:** 26*t*, 54/55, 65, 69, 83, 106, 113*b*, 114. **Mozart-Gedenkstätte Augsburg:** pages 41*t b*, 88, 107. **Museum der Stadt Baden:** page 91. **Bild-Archiv der Österreichischen Nationalbibliothek, Wien:** pages 9, 17, 27*t*, 31*tr*, 37, 38*b*, 46, 51*t*, 57, 64, 72, 74, 77*t*, 86, 92, 98, 109, 113*t*. **J Pierpont Morgan Collection, New York:** page 26*b*. **Royal College of Music, London:** 36, 61, 66, 68, 76, 81, 85, 93, 108, 110, 115, 122. **Stadtbibliothek, Vienna:** page 100. **Stift St Peter, Salzburg:** page 33*t*. **Theater-Museum, Munich:** page 52*b*.

The author wishes to acknowledge her debt to many sources. Of the vast amount of literature on Mozart, the following will be found invaluable.

Emily Anderson, ed.: *The Letters of Mozart and his Family* (London, 1938; revised 1966)

Peter J Davies: 'Mozart's Illnesses and Death', *The Musical Times*, cxxv (1984)

E J Dent: *Mozart's Operas: A Critical Study* (London, 1913; 2nd edition, 1947)

Otto Erich Deutsch: *Mozart und seine Welt in zeitgenössischen Bildern* (iconography; Kassel, 1961; in German and English)

Albert Einstein: *Mozart, his Character, his Work* (English translation, New York, 1945)

Carolyn Gianturco: *Mozart's Early Operas* (London, 1981)

W Hildesheimer: *Mozart* (Frankfurt am Main, 1977; English translation, 1979)

Arthur Hutchings: *A Companion to Mozart's Piano Concertos* (London, 1956; 2nd edition, 1965)

Ludwig von Kochel: *Chronologisch-thematisches Verzeichnis sämtlicher Tonwerke Wolfgang Amade Mozarts* (Leipzig, 1862; 6th edition, 1964)

Nigel Lewis: *Paperchase: Mozart, Beethoven, Bach...The Search for Their Lost Music* (London, 1981)

William Mann: *The Operas of Mozart* (London, 1977)

Charles Osborne: *The Complete Operas of Mozart* (London, 1978)

H C Robbins Landon: *1791: Mozart's Last Year* (London, 1988)

H C Robbins Landon and Donald Mitchell: *The Mozart Companion* (London, 1956; 2nd edition, 1965)

Stanley Sadie: *Mozart* (London, 1966)

Stanley Sadie: 'Mozart', *The New Grove Dictionary of Music and Musicians* (London, 1980; offprint with revisions, 1986)

The front and back endpapers reproduce one of the last pages of Mozart's own thematic catalogue of his works, showing Die Zauberflöte, La clemenza di Tito, *the* Clarinet Concerto *and* Eine kleine Freimaurer-Kantate.

Im Jullius.

Die Zauberflöte. — — nachgesetzt den 30.t September
— — eine teutsche Oper in 2 Aufzügen. von Emm: Schikaneder.
bestehend in 22 Stücken. — Sängerinen. — Mad:elle Gottlieb. Mad:me Hofer. Mad:e Görl.
Mad:me Klöpfer. und Md:elle Hofmann. Männer. Hr. Schack. Hr. Görl. Hr. Schikaneder der ältere.
Hr. Müller. Hr. Schikaneder der jüngere. Hr. Nouseul. — Chör.

Den 5.t September. — nachgesetzt in Prag den 6.t September.
La Clemenza di Tito opera seria in due Atti. per l'incoro=
nazione di sua maestá l'imperatore Leopoldo II. — ridotta á
vera opera dal sig:re Mazzolá: Poeta di sua A: S: l'Elettore di
Saßonia. — _Attrici_: — Sig:ra Marchetti fantozi. — Sig:ra Antonini.
— Attori. Sig:r Bedini. Sig:ra Carolina Perini /dall'omo/ Sig:r
Baglioni. Sig:r Campi. — e Cori. — 24 Pezzi.

den 28.t September.
zur Oper. die _Zauberflöte_ — einen Priestermarsch und die ouvertur.

Ein konzert für die Clarinette. für Hr. Stadler den ältern.
begleitung. 2 violin, viola, 2 flaute, 2 fagotti, 2 Corni e Baßi.

den 15.t November.

Eine kleine freymäurer=kantate. bestehend aus 1 Chor. 1 Arie.
2 Recitativen, und ein Duo. tenor und Baß.
2 violin, viola, Baßi, 1 flauto, 2 obe e 2 Corni. —